MAMI
My Grandmother's Journey

GOLD MOUNTAIN STORIES

A series co-published by the Chinese Canadian Historical Society of British Columbia and the Initiative for Student Research and Teaching in Chinese Canadian Studies.

Series Editors: Jean Wilson and Henry Yu
Managing Editor: Jennifer L Yip
Advisory Board: Jean Barman, Jennifer Chen, Victor Ho,
David Lai, Chris Lee, Karin Lee, Colleen Leung, Peter Li, Imogene Lim,
Patricia Roy, Jan Walls, Jean Wilson, Andrew Yang, Paul Yee, Henry Yu

Rebeca Lau, *Mami: My Grandmother's Journey*
Chad Reimer, *Chilliwack's Chinatowns: A History*

MAMI
My Grandmother's Journey

Rebeca Lau

Chinese Canadian Historical Society of British Columbia

and

Initiative for Student Teaching and Research
in Chinese Canadian Studies,
University of British Columbia

Vancouver, BC

This book is published by the Chinese Canadian Historical Society of British Columbia (CCHSBC) and the Initiative for Student Teaching and Research in Chinese Canadian Studies (INSTRCC) with permission of the author.

INSTRCC
University of British Columbia
http://www.instrcc.ubc.ca

   UBC's Initiative for Student Teaching and Research in Chinese Canadian studies (INSTRCC) has been built from the ground up by students collaborating with committed faculty and community groups. It focuses on recovering the rich and complex story of "Pacific Canada" as a geographical and historical concept.

CCHSBC
http://www.cchsbc.ca

   Founded in 2004, through its four-fold mandate of research, documentation, preservation and education, the Chinese Canadian Historical Society of BC (CCHSBC) seeks to tell the history of the Chinese community in BC.

Library and Archives Canada Cataloguing in Publication

Lau, Rebeca, 1968-
    Mami : my grandmother's journey / Rebeca Lau.

Co-published by: Initiative for Student Teaching and Research in
    Chinese Canadian Studies, University of British Columbia.
ISBN 978-0-9783420-5-0

    1. Chong de Lau, Mami, 1930-2007. 2. Chinese--Mexico--Tapachula
(Chiapas)--Biography. 3. Tapachula (Chiapas, Mexico)--Biography.
4. China--Biography. I. Chinese Canadian Historical Society of British
Columbia II. Title.

F1256.L39 2010   972'.75   C2010-904725-7

Printed in Canada

To Mami and Teti, Ah-Popo and Ah-Kung
I know you are always with me

CONTENTS

FOREWORD

Today an estimated 40,000,000 persons Chinese by birth or descent live outside of China itself. Three-quarters do so elsewhere in Asia, the other quarter is spread out around the world. Chinese emigration goes back many centuries in time. Initially it was primarily within Asia, but between the mid-1800s and mid-1900s over 6,000,000 Chinese left their homeland for Canada and the United States, Australia and New Zealand, Western Europe, and Latin America including Brazil, Peru, Cuba, and Mexico.

Whereas Chinese overseas are now for the most part recognized for their contributions to the societies to which they come, such was not always the case. Until recently, Chinese in search of a better life for themselves and also to support their families back home were often viewed with suspicion for taking away jobs and also for differences in appearance and behaviour. Chinese immigrants had to be resourceful and resilient to survive and thrive. Lack of understanding in host countries long obscured their contributions.

It has taken a new generation of writers to turn traditional attitudes on their head. Rather than viewing Chinese overseas as usurpers, they have sought to understand their circumstances and to value their lives. Many authors are themselves Chinese, sometimes the sons and daughters, grandsons and granddaughters, of earlier immigrants. These authors' ability to write both from a familial perspective and from that of the receiving society in which they themselves have grown up gives those accounts a particular force and authority. Among their number in Canada are Denise Chong's *The Concubine's Children* (1995), Wayson Choy's *Paper Shadows* (1999), Colleen Leung's documentary *Letters from Home* (2001), and Judy Fong Bates' *The Year of Finding Memory* (2010).

Some overseas Chinese, as with Rebeca Lau, bring not a double but a triple gaze to their writing. Not only their families, but they themselves cross national boundaries. Rebeca is among 1,200,000 persons Chinese by descent now living in Canada, 400,000 of them like her in British Columbia. By virtue of her birth and upbringing, she is also among an estimated 23,000 Mexicans who are Chinese by descent.

I have had the privilege of knowing Rebeca Lau since she began her graduate studies at the University of British Columbia. Her interest in family history caused her so to focus her thesis, which I supervised. It was from this beginning that *Mami: My Grandmother's Journey* sprang.

In her quest for understanding, Rebeca Lau has drawn on the insights that come from her education in the United States and residence in Vancouver with its large Chinese population, some of whose families arrived upwards to a century and a half ago. The presence of so many others in similar circumstances made it much more natural for her to want to explore how it was that grandparents and parents took their courage in their hands and acted as they did in sometimes difficult circumstances.

In *Mami: My Grandmother's Journey*, Rebeca Lau invites us along as she returns to what is still "home" after almost two decades away. In Tapachula, on the west coast of Mexico bordering Guatemala, Mami reminisces about a family history going back to 1919 even as she cooks up a storm to ensure her granddaughter tastes the entirety of Chinese and Mexican delicacies familiar from her early years. The complexities of belonging and not belonging to both China and Mexico, in Rebeca's case also to Canada, become clearer to her as she also explores the multi-generational family compound built around a general store, talks with longtime Chinese families clustered nearby, and visits childhood haunts. The result is a kind of adventure story, highly readable even as it embodies deeper meaning as it narrates the experiences of three generations of Chinese making their lives on the southern edge of Mexico.

Mami: My Grandmother's Journey is one family's story among the millions to be told by Chinese overseas. It is only comparatively recently, with Lynn Pan's *Sons of the Yellow Emperor* (1990) and Philip Kuhn's *Chinese Among Others* (2008), that the emphasis has shifted to seeing Chinese abroad as part of an ongoing international phenomenon with multiple origins and destinations, rather than seeing them solely within the context of the country to which they came. Rebeca Lau's triple gaze contributes to this new direction by virtue of situating her family across the generations not in a single place but as moving between multiple "homes" for economic, educational, and personal reasons.

Rebeca Lau's journey toward understanding resonates for Chinese in Canada and around the world -- and indeed for all of us whose families come from away. Many of us find ourselves knowing far less about our inheritance than we thought we did and often do not have the tools, or so we think, to find out more. Rebeca was determined to respect her grandmother, who is at the heart of the book, but not at the expense of sentimentalizing her story. Much like Mami, her granddaughter dared to challenge the unknown and gives us the courage also to do so. We come to realize that it is not in the grand discoveries of names, dates, and events but in the shared intimacy of everyday life that the past becomes part of who we are in the present day going forward into the future. *Mami: My Grandmother's Journey* gives encouragement to those of us – of Chinese descent or not – curious about our own histories.

Jean Barman

ACKNOWLEDGEMENTS

Mami: My Grandmother's Journey was never intended for publication. When Mami talked about us writing a book about her life, I imagined it as nothing more than a coilbound class project and that it would remain hidden as a family treasure at best. So when I sent the first draft to Jean Barman I only meant for her to suggest edits so that the piece would be more readable. Then I would head to the nearest Kinko's to bind it, distribute it to members of the Lau family, and declare it a "mission accomplished" to Mami.

Many years and edits later, it has become the book that Mami and I fantasized over while eating our favourite sweetbreads on a hot November day in Tapachula. Even more, it has become a "publication," the real thing, something I never envisioned but am enormously grateful for. Many wonderful believers and supporters played an essential part in the realization of this project; this wasn't just my doing.

Thank you, Jean Barman, for encouraging me to "just write…" for patiently suggesting edits, after edits, after edits, and for nudging me to pursue this fantasy with excitement and passion. It is because of you that we can finally use the "b" (book) word.

Huge thanks to David Stephens, Bill French, Evelyn Hu-Dehart, Roberto Ham Chande, Silvia Martínez Treviño, Neil

Guppy, Judy Maxwell, Carlos Lau Camacho, Elda Reyes de Lau, and everyone in the Chinese Community in Tapachula. You have given me endless inspiration and encouragement.

I am indebted to Henry Yu, the Initiative for Student Teaching and Research in Chinese Canadian Studies, and the Chinese Canadian Historical Society of British Columbia for the unique opportunity of presenting this as a formal piece of work and opening the path of discovery. Jennifer Yip coordinated production of the book. The design for the book was the work of Jacqueline Wang. Brendan Albano created www.rebecalau.com. And special thanks to Jean Wilson for your expertise and insights into book publishing, and for your objectivity and passion matched with tact, warmth, and patience.

I appreciate the immeasurable support from all my friends in Vancouver and all over Mexico. You know who you are. Thank you for always being there for me.

For their unconditional love and acceptance, I am extremely grateful to my parents, Carlos Luis and Michele Rebecca, to my sisters Guada and Vero, to Dagmar and Kjell in Sweden, to Guy, Luisfe, and Nico in Montreal, to my family in various parts of Mexico. Words are just not enough…

And to Pälle, my husband, best friend, and a blind believer in everything I do. TQMM.

MAMI

My Grandmother's Journey

THE YOUNGEST
OF SIXTEEN

AIRPORTS are bittersweet places where longed-for encounters and painful goodbyes take place. But today there is no time for people-watching as I run vigorously from International Arrivals to Domestic Departures in the *Aeropuerto Internacional de México*, trying to make it on time for my connecting and final flight to Tapachula.

Earlier this morning in Vancouver, I began this journey to meet up with my grandma, Mami. She is flying in from Campeche, where she has been living with her daughter and my aunt, Tía Lupe. Together, we will spend over two weeks in Casa Lau, which has not been lived in for a few years since Mami permanently moved to Campeche.

I am breathless and can feel drops of perspiration running down my spine and across my forehead, but I make it on time for my flight. Mami is sitting in the first row right after business class, waiting and fidgeting nervously. She gives me a huge smile as soon as she sees me. I hug her and kiss her on the cheek and then make sure she has her safety belt correctly strapped. Then I sit down and buckle up as well, while Mami tells me that she had warned the entire crew that she would have to give them a piece of her mind if they left without her granddaughter, who was coming all the way from Canada. I simply shake my head, *"Ay, Mami,"* and tell her that, as she can see, there is no need to get all frazzled just as we feel the plane moving away from the gate and hear the flight attendant's voice giving safety instructions. We are leaving Mexico City on time.

Mami looks great. She is a small-framed, dark-haired woman with fair-coloured soft skin and no make-up. Her hair, which is straight, thin, and short with hardly noticeable gray, used to be long, dark, and worn in a braid. I do not recall when she had it cut off, but I remember seeing her thick braid all rolled up in the bureau next to her bed. She wears sunglasses because her cataracts make her eyes quite sensitive to the light.

She has always liked the heat and, and as she has gotten older, gets cold more easily. She reminds me in Chinese that she is afraid of being cold, *"Ngo hou pa tong."* Therefore she wears layers of clothing: wool undergarments, one long-sleeved blouse, two thin sweaters, and a vest. She is also wearing long johns, wool long pants, and two pairs of socks. I am only wearing a t-shirt and baggy cotton pants since it is close to 28 degrees. I feel the heat just looking at her but say nothing about it and ask her to let me know if she gets any colder so I can get her my fleece sweater, which is easily accessible in my backpack.

People have always said to me that I look more like Mami (who was born in China) and her eldest daughter (my aunt, Tía Chony) than either of my parents. In fact, when I was younger and living in Tapachula, I often heard somebody yelling *"Hola, Chony"* when I ran an errand around town. In return, I would simply wave and give a broad smile. Now, sitting next to Mami, I realize we have the same elongated face and forehead and flat nose and share a preference for no make-up and comfortable clothes. Like Mami, I have a small frame that got me known as *flaca* or *hueso*, skinny or bone, throughout my school years. Nicknaming was so normal when I was growing up that even now I can easily recall friends' nicknames and have difficulty remembering their proper names.

I am, however, taller than Mami, something that everyone says I inherited from both my grandfather and my father. Also, my skin is darker, which often provokes the question of whether I come from Malaysia or Singapore; no one ever suspects I am from Mexico. And unlike Mami, I depend on prescription glasses to see the world around me (I am nearsighted and have worn them since I was seventeen).

Mami says to me in Spanish that she does not care about things that are *a la moda* or in fashion. Most of her clothes she sewed herself of cotton or polyester fabrics twenty-five or even thirty years ago. But in the last few years, she has asked my parents to buy her new clothes when they go to Hong Kong. She says nowhere else in the world do they make clothes the way she likes them. Hong Kong is the only place where the patterns, the colours, and the sizes suit her perfectly. So she has replaced the majority of her home-sewn dresses with store-bought baggy blouses and dark pants with elastic waistbands (nothing tight or constraining because feeling comfortable is more important than looking fashionable).

As we take off, Mami turns to me and asks, *"Nei chi mchi tou tinkai neitei kiu gnotei 'mami' 'teti' ah?"* ("Do you know why you call us 'Mami' and 'Teti'?"). I have heard this story a few times but Mami does not let me answer and continues talking.

"Teti had sent your uncles and aunts to Kowloon to study Chinese; and when they returned, they began to call us 'Mami' and 'Teti.' You little girls copied whatever your uncles and aunts did and repeated everything they said. No matter how often we all corrected you, you three girls kept calling us 'Mami' and 'Teti' instead of the proper *Ah-Mah* and *Ah-Yeh*." This time she adds to her story: "To tell you the truth, I never minded; in fact, your grandfather liked it and so do I. I wonder what your parents thought of this." It was not until I was in my teens studying in the United States that it dawned on me that the word *Mami* meant "Mommy" and *Teti* meant "Daddy." My parents have always been *Mamita* and *Papito*, or *Ma* and *Papi*.

Mami speaks a Chinese dialect from Kau Kong called *Kau Kong Wah* and considers it her mother tongue. Chinese is the language she is most comfortable with in spite of the fact that she says she has forgotten a lot of words and thinks her expressions are antiquated, having lived in Mexico for so long and unable to keep up with the latest Chinese slang.

She speaks Spanish as well but, likes to call herself a *media lengua* ("a half-tongue"), a term she has coined to reflect her thinking that her vocabulary is limited and that she has nothing to talk about with others in Spanish. She avoids situations that would force her into any serious or not so serious conversations beyond *buenos días, ¿cómo está?* (common salutations). Her Spanish audience is pretty small: a few neighbours, a salesperson here and there, a waiter in a restaurant, a caller looking for my aunt, a repairperson coming to fix something. When she speaks Spanish, she does it with a Chinese accent, converting mid-word r's into l's, skipping the last consonant in a word so plurals become obsolete, forgetting the right verb conjugations, or simply shortening her sentences and avoiding annoying, monosyllabic *la* and *el* pronouns. *¿Cómo 'ta?* is really *¿Cómo estás?* and *Calo* is *Carlos*, the name for almost every male in this side of the family from Teti (Carlos), to Papito (Carlos Luis), to my uncles (Carlos, Juan Carlos), one of my cousins (Carlos), and even Tía Lupe's husband (Carlos Humberto).

Mixing Chinese and Spanish is something Mami tends to do, sometimes on purpose and mostly unknowingly. When she converses with other *paisanos*, who may also speak both Chinese and Spanish, one can hear a few Spanish words thrown in here and there. As in any language, there are words in Spanish that cannot be translated into Chinese, and vice versa, as they either do not convey the same idea or simply do not exist. And when she interacts with a Spanish-speaking neighbour, she adds a few Chinese words, unaware that sometimes she leaves her conversation partner confused. She also uses the same "loud" voice and "harsh" tone when she speaks Chinese as when she speaks Spanish, making any listener unfamiliar with the cacophony of the Chinese language think that Mami is always scolding everyone or trying to win a debate.

She can still read Chinese, however, as long as it is written in big characters, and she regrets, only slightly, not liking school when she was younger and lovingly putting a little bit of blame on her father. "He was a good man, but he spoiled me because…" She smiles and switches to Spanish, *"po' que yo era su consentida"* ("because I was his favourite child"). Then she continues in Kau Kong dialect. "He was so harsh with all the other kids he taught, including his own sons. My father treated his only two daughters better than his boys, which was not common for Chinese tradition, where schooling was usually for boys."

"When I was growing up, it was unusual for girls to go to school because we were destined to be given away; so there was no need to educate us. When girls get married, they no longer belong to their parents because they become part of their husband's family. But my older sister, sister #11, knew how to read and was educated because she liked learning, and my father was a teacher who loved us girls more than the boys."

"But when it came down to me, my father would let me do anything I wanted. And since I was not interested in school, I was allowed to run freely and spend my days playing. This is why I don't know that many characters and still don't know how to write Chinese."

Time goes by quickly and I suddenly see from the airplane window the different shades of green colours marking the thick, lush, tropical vegetation. There is a rich assortment of palm and coconut trees below as well as mango trees and banana plantations. As we descend a bit more, we also enjoy watching from above the beautiful, blue hues of the Pacific Ocean and the whiteness of the waves as they hit the shoreline.

Mami was born in Cha Ping Si, Yan Yeong Seh, in a small district of Kau Kong, in Guangdong, southern China, a place she refers to as her parents' home.

"*¿Cuántos años tiene, mami?*" ("How old are you, Mami?"), I ask her.

"No sé" ("I don't know."), she answers, looking at me with sharp black eyes and then adds in Spanish with a familiar Chinese accent, *"¿Po' qué me pregunta?"* ("Why do you ask?"). She explains that birthdays, especially for girls, were not something important to remember or celebrate.

"There were no birthday parties or gifts to constantly remind me of or make me look forward to this date. Age was not something people asked us when we were growing up." She pauses to think and calculates she was born some eighty years ago. It was not until recently that she knew this piece of information about herself. Her nephew, Paco, living in Hong Kong had written her a letter with her exact date of birth, according to a family tree he had gotten found.

I listen intensely without really understanding because the date is according to the Chinese calendar. The only thing I pick up is that her birthday is on the fourth month and on the twenty-sixth day of the Chinese calendar. She smiles with satisfaction, and at that moment I realize that the date is not as important as the feeling of pride she has in knowing when she was born and having it written down to show me.

Out of sixteen kids, Mami is the youngest of the family. She says that, like her age, she never really knew her parents' names. "I think my father's name was Ming Chiu. I heard people calling him Ah-Ming. And my older sister told me that my mother's name was Po Chiu. It was not like somebody would tell me these things. What if everybody knew each other?"

Her father was a respected and well-known man, one of the teachers in town. His first wife and their first-born, a baby girl, both died during the delivery. After this unfortunate event, her father remarried. Mami's mother was the second wife; she had fifteen children and stayed home to care for them and the household. Of the sixteen children (Mami counts all children born from both "Big Mother" and "Second Mother"), seven died when they were born. Of the nine who survived, Mami and her sister #11 were the only girls in the house.

Mami remembers some things here and there from her childhood. Her mother was very caring and had young girls help her with the house chores in exchange for room and board, a gesture that poorer families welcomed. The majority of these girls grew up as part of Mami's family and were called *yeung noi*.

Mami recalls playing outdoors like a tomboy and learning crafts at home (the only thing she acknowledges she enjoyed) from other girls and women in the neighbourhood. She also remembers her father teaching many kids and her mother doing chores around the house. And she has vague memories of her brothers studying with her father and then later leaving the household.

She is saddened by the fact that memories of her parents, her brothers, and sister #11 are limited simply because she did not spend much time, if any, with them individually or as a family unit. She sighs and says that was just the way things were. But the one thing she carries with her from her younger years is the memory of her father. With tears in her eyes Mami talks about him.

"No matter what I did or didn't do, I could do no wrong in my father's eyes. When he saw me, his expression always softened and I was the centre of his attention. I don't think he knew how much I treasured him and I really regret never having been able to show him how much I appreciated him."

After what seems a long cry, she turns to me with red eyes and says, "I'm glad I still remember him." She cannot describe to me what he looked like, but she tells me he was kind and respected, and he loved his two daughters, especially Mami, something that she emphasizes was very unusual for a Chinese man of that time and place.

2

AN ARRANGED MARRIAGE

TAPACHULA is the last major metropolitan area before Guatemala. The distance between Tapachula and the Mexico-Guatemala border is approximately thirty kilometres. It is hot and humid and considered remote and not easily accessible because it is bordered by rivers, jungle, and mountainous terrain to the west, north, and east and by the Pacific Ocean to the south. Looking northbound (northeast, really), one can see the majestic *volcán Tacaná*.

Because of its remoteness and the difficulty of access, Tapachula's growth and "progress" came at a slow but steady pace (its natural beauty remaining untouched for many centuries until the early 1900s). It began as a cattle-producing and agricultural area (cotton, cocoa, coffee beans, and tropical fruits such as bananas, papayas, and pineapples) and was inhabited by a culturally-rich, self-reliant, indigenous population.

Only in the late nineteenth and early twentieth centuries did contact with the outside world impact this small city, causing it to become a commercial hub with an international flavour that included immigrants from Central America, Spain, Germany, China, Japan (and in smaller numbers, Turkey, France, and England). The Port of San Benito was built in the early 1800s, and Tapachula's railroad connection was finished in 1908.

Tapachula is now a bustling, charming, medium-sized city of about 190,000 inhabitants, and as we arrive I smell the humidity and heat mixed with something else I cannot describe but that makes me realize I have returned home. I was born and raised here until the age of seventeen and still feel a special connection to this place.

The "new" airport is larger than the one we had when I was little. The old one was quaint and small, all on one floor with no separate waiting gates or airconditioning. It was painted white and blue, quite open with lots of flowers, and it was about ten minutes from the city. The building itself was one open area with rows of fixed hard-plastic, round-bottomed blue chairs where people congregated to wait for departing flights and at the same time welcomed visitors and returning travellers. At one end there was a large opening with a cement counter, where after arriving one would pick up luggage upon showing a claim ticket. Nearby were two check-in desks where seats were assigned using numbered stickers; closer to the tarmac there was a small sit-down cafeteria that served sandwiches, cakes, cold drinks, and local coffee, open only once a day around noon when the only flight arrived and departed for Mexico City, stopping in Tuxtla Gutiérrez and then Villahermosa along the way. With one flight per day, the airport was not used often, but I think it really suited Tapachula, what we call our *pueblo*.

The "newer" airport looks more austere and darker. It is an enclosed building with brown tinted windows, waxed floors, a full-blast central airconditioning system, and a couple of small shops opposite the airline check-in counters. It is built on two floors and has a restaurant on top where one can watch the runway. There are two separate arrival and departure gates. Since Tapachula is a border city and an entry point into Mexico, the *salidas* gate has mandatory customs and immigration checkpoints before one enters the check-in counter area. Since there is no longer a flight between Guatemala and Mexico City, it is common to leave Central America by land and then fly out from Tapachula. Therefore, one can hear different Guatemalan and Salvadorean accents in addition to the chattering of Mexican passengers. The separate *llegadas* area has an actual conveyor belt and leads into a welcoming area where people wait for their loved ones to surface.

A temperature of 38° Celsius welcomes us with a humidity level of almost 100%. Having refused a wheelchair, Mami walks slowly down the metal stairway with a bulky black purse hanging over her head and shoulder. She does not go anywhere without this purse because it is where she keeps all her medication. As well, she always carries a black leather bag strapped around her waist where she says she can have easier access to things she needs right away such as Kleenex tissue, a few honey and lemon-flavoured Hall's coughdrops, a comb, a wallet with some bills and coins, and house keys. She has made a string out of an old dress she no longer uses and has threaded a set of keys through it, which hang around her neck so that she is never locked out of the house.

"I'm alone most of the day, so I need to remember to have keys on me at all times. This string," she shows and proudly explains to me, "is made of cotton and does not give me rashes since sometimes it can get quite hot in the house."

As I look at the string, I question when was the last time I used my hands to convert anything useless into something useful instead of running to the store and simply buying what I needed. Ashamed, I realize it has been too long ago for me to even begin to recall that sense of pride and accomplishment Mami is showing me.

But I brush off that feeling of inferiority and focus on helping Mami with the task at hand. As we descend the stairway, she holds onto the handrail with her right hand, the one normally reserved for Grandpa Teti's old wooden cane for support. I recall Teti buying this bamboo cane at a souvenir shop in San Francisco's Chinatown on a trip they had taken me on when I was little. At the bottom of the staircase, I hand her back Teti's bamboo cane, which she accepts, though

I still hold onto her left arm. We feel the intense heat, smell the engine fumes, and are disoriented by the high-pitched sound of the plane, so we focus on slowly walking along the tarmac beside and around the plane towards the *llegadas* glass door.

"Mami, how did you and Teti meet?"

"We had matchmakers," Mami starts explaining. "We could not choose a groom or go out on a date. In my case, I did not decide or even know I was getting married. My parents decided I had reached the age to get married; then my mother and close older female relatives invited the matchmaker to have tea and discuss all my personal information."

The matchmaker was usually an older, well-respected woman in the community. According to tradition, the matchmaker would write everything on a red piece of paper and would keep tabs on who was ready for marriage and the attributes each family was looking for. It was not just two people getting married; the union was between two families. So everything about the families was important to consider. The boy's family wanted to know about any illness or diseases in the girl's family, their wealth, any jobs that had been held among the closest relatives, the family's place in society and its reputation, as well as the girls' habits, skills, and attitudes.

I had heard things like this while I was growing up, usually while eavesdropping on the adults' conversations. But I was never sure of their entire meaning as they spoke fast and sometimes in a different dialect or used words I was not familiar with. Also, when they talked and reminisced, they would only speak in half sentences (assuming that their listeners knew the exact meaning of what they were referring to). I also heard bits and pieces about the way things were "in China when I was little…" when Mami would say how lucky I was to be born in Mexico. But I had not paid that much attention because most of the time this was an introduction to being scolded. So I am now intrigued to hear Mami talk about her "arranged marriage" in such detail.

"A boy's family would look for the girl's abilities to cook, clean the house, take care of her husband and his family. It would be best if the girl did not smoke, drink, or do drugs; she could not be a tomboy or opinionated either. She should be respectful, loyal, delicate, and quiet."

"My father wasn't very involved in looking for my future husband. He probably had spoken with my mother, so it was her responsibility to look after this. My mother would get the names of a few prospects from the matchmaker and also would ask around if anybody knew of a boy wanting to get married. Then she would get into conversations with the neighbours or a shopkeeper and ask discreetly about the boy's family, and she would know which families were good or bad. But it was the boy and his family who realistically and ultimately chose the bride and her family."

"The groom-to-be had many chances to look and inquire

Mami and Teti in a trip to Esquipulas, Guatemala (late 1970s).

about a girl and her family. His family would meet the matchmaker and give her *lai-see* (a red envelope with lucky money) every time the boy wanted to take a look at a girl. Then, his family would also request the matchmaker for a prospective girl's red paper and would ask around about the girl and her family. The girl would be sent out on errands, and the matchmaker would let the boy know where the girl would be so he would have as many chances as he wanted to see her (though he could never approach her). His family would also rely on the matchmaker's opinions as well as the advice of a fortune teller to determine if the families would be compatible."

"Once the boy liked what he saw and his family was satisfied with her family history, his family would then invite the girl's family for a tea ceremony at his home. The girl's father, mother, and only the married women in her family could attend...like the women who were married to my older brothers. Then they would all choose a proper date for the wedding." She sighs and adds, "We girls never had the chance to look at any boys and choose. Being a girl, I would never even know that a certain boy was looking at me to be his bride. I was never present during the meetings with the matchmaker either."

"One day, I was just told that in a week I would get married. And from that time until the wedding, I was locked in one room in the house where female relatives and girlfriends took turns keeping me company and bringing me food (I could have no male visitors at all). I spent all seven days before my wedding in this room where I was entertained, had meals served to me, washed myself, and slept. I do not remember the details during this week but only that was the one time in my life when I was the focus of so much attention and care from female family members, my mother's girlfriends, and neighbours."

I listen to Mami with a mixture of feelings. I envy the ceremonious ways of how a husband was chosen for her, which I understand to be about how important this was to her family as well as to the culmination of this major rite of passage. I pay attention to the details and am curious about the meaning and intention behind them and try to envision each part everyone played to make this happen and what an enormous responsibility was placed on the parents and the matchmaker to bring about the successful union of two people and two families.

On the other hand, I feel fortunate and empowered that I had a say in the decision about spending my life with a person I got to know and love. I met my husband-to-be in an ESL class in university and five years later, without being sequestered for seven days, we got married in front of a Justice of the Peace. But regardless of the process, I realize that both Mami and I ended up marrying the right man, and that the process does not diminish that important fact.

3

RETURNING
TO CASA LAU

AS we enter the baggage claim area, I see Tío Carlos and Tía Elda, my uncle and his wife, happily waving at us through the thick glass from the *llegadas* area. I do the same and smile back. They drove to the airport from their home on *la novena* (9th Avenue) to welcome us and to take us to Casa Lau. While we make our way through the crowds waiting for their luggage to appear on the conveyor belt, I ask Mami which pieces are hers so I can take them. She has only one suitcase because she keeps some clothes in Casa Lau so she does not need to pack very much for each visit from Campeche. Once we have everything, I notice Tío Carlos telling the guard that he is only coming into the restricted area to help me get the luggage.

"Doña Mari, ¿cómo ha estado?" Tío Carlos says effusively to Mami and embraces her at the same time. Then Tío Carlos and I give each other a big hug while he says, *"Huachijul"* and I respond, *"Mashkut."* I still do not know the meaning, much less the spelling, of these two words, but Teti used them frequently and learned a lot of other words from his

various *indígenas* customers coming from the *fincas*, from Guatemala, from *la sierra*, and the surrounding towns. I cannot recall how, when, or why Tío Carlos and I began using this greeting, but these two words have just stuck with us. I am pretty certain Tío Carlos does not know what *mashkut* and *huachijul* mean either.

I hand Mami her bamboo cane back, and she walks in front of us as we drag all the pieces while the guard makes sure the tickets we are holding match the tags attached to each piece of luggage. When we are finally allowed to exit, we meet up with Tía Elda, who also welcomes us warmly. She then assists Mami to the car while we wheel the luggage to the open-air parkade and chitchat on our way. We load up Tío Carlos' Pontiac four-door sedan and take the new divided four-lane highway into the city.

On our way in, I just sit, listen, smell, and look at the astounding changes in the cityscape. Tapachula has grown so much that residential areas have appeared in the middle of what used to be large fields of cotton, ranches, and lush vegetation. Where there used to be a narrow two-way semi-deserted rural road linking the port and beaches of Puerto Madero to the airport and ending in Tapachula, there is now a busy highway with two lanes in each direction separated by a median. The city has expanded past the old outskirts into new *colonias* and streets where there were only *monte* (outgrown fields) before.

I am surprised to see the latest models of Nissans, Toyotas, Hondas, and other foreign cars loaded with the latest gadgets. When I was growing up, vehicle choices within Mexico and more so in Tapachula were limited and reduced to Volkswagens, Renaults, Chevrolets, Fords, and Dodges. The most luxurious car was perhaps a Cadillac, and it was a rarity and extremely expensive to have airconditioning, power windows, leather, or automatic transmission.

For the longest time, many side streets remained unpaved, and the paved ones had potholes here and there. But now, as we drive in, all the dusty quiet roads have become highly circulated paved streets. When I was growing up, there were horse-drawn carriages, men pulling carts, tricycles, even horses and burros sharing the roads with cars and beat-up trucks, not SUV's and the newer cars I now see on the road. I am surprised to see Burger King and large chain stores like Chedraui, Aurrera, and Fábricas de Francia. People used to eat at family-run local restaurants and shop at *tiendas de abarrotes* or small mom-and-pop grocery stores for foods.

Because of all the changes in traffic direction, we now drive in a big loop to get to Casa Lau. In the old days, in the smaller Tapachula, it was a lot easier to get around because the city was divided into four sections by one *central* avenue going north-south and another one running east-west (with even numbers of avenues going one way and odd numbers of streets the other way). Also, sections would have *avenidas* (avenues) that would usually go north-south and *calles* (streets) that would normally run east-west. With the recent growth in and around Tapachula, I am not surprised to read street names that sound unfamiliar to me.

Casa Lau is located on the corner of *la octava norte* (North 8th Avenue) and *la treceava poniente* (West 13th Street). Our house is on top of Casa Lau, the small grocery store that Teti opened a few years after he arrived in Tapachula as a young man on his own in 1919. As we park in front of our big, silver *portón*, I quickly scan the street and realize that some of the businesses have now changed as well. *La octava norte* used to be the street known for its Chinese-owned grocery stores, but most of those stores have disappeared and other businesses have sprouted up in their place.

Tío Carlos removes the thick chain and solid padlock that keep Casa Lau safe from intruders while it sits empty. He then hands me the whole set of keys marked Casa Lau. Before he even has time to remind me which key opens the top lock and which key is for the bottom lock, I have already opened the side door of the *portón* that has always been used as the main entrance. I hold on to Mami's arm and help her get over and down a high step into the building.

The large metal *portón* that goes from ceiling to floor was intended to be a garage entrance, and briefly my father, Papito, used this space to store his first car, which was also our first family automobile, a blue Volkswagen beetle. But that plan was short-lived because during the rainy season, water from the street easily flowed along the low sidewalk and slipped underneath the *portón*. After many failed attempts to keep the water from coming in, Papito built up the outside sidewalk and at the same time added a higher threshold, converting this area into much-needed storage where we kept fifty-kilogram sacks of sugar and empty boxes for repacking sold goods for the grocery store. Then, he decided to lease a space in a family-run parking lot that had covered individual stalls a block and a half away from home. We used that as a parking space for many years.

As we walk in, I notice that there are now solid concrete walls where the door to the store and the doors that led to the two warehouses used to be. I feel claustrophobic since the area looks much smaller than what I remember and is full of boxes marked with my aunts' names that contain their personal belongings, collecting dust and spider webs.

It suddenly hits me with an unexplainable harshness and sadness that the business side of Casa Lau that I remember from my childhood is no longer there and has not been for a little over ten years. Instead of Teti's grocery store, the current tenants opened up a *ferretería* where they sell construction, plumbing, and some electrical materials. I feel a slight ache in my heart and dismiss it, trying as much as I can to take all the changes in stride.

From the hallway, a yellow concrete staircase leads from

the warehouse and the store to what was our second-floor house. Tía Elda takes Mami's arm and helps her go upstairs. At the top, Mami unlocks the big wooden entrance door, while Tío Carlos and I remove the luggage from the car and carry it up.

About ten steps before I arrive at the wooden door, I suddenly realize that the barbershop on the opposite side of the street is no longer there. For as long as I can remember, this was where Teti and Papito went to get their haircuts and, once in a while, a shave. *El peluquero* was a slim and well-mannered man with thin frizzy hair who owned and ran this small barbershop, which was opened for long hours and closed only on Sunday afternoons. It had two high red chairs and a large mirror, which directly faced our *portón*. From our yellow staircase, we could see the mirror in the shop and the reflection of the back of whoever was standing outside our *portón* ringing the bell. This is how we knew if it was safe to open the door. Without the barber and his mirror, we will now have to yell *"¿quién es?"* from the inside before opening the main door.

Since Tío Carlos had hired a person to clean the staircase, living room, dining room, and kitchen, Mami and I will only have to clean her old room (where we will stay) and her bathroom as well as the few dishes and pots we will be using. We begin by opening up the large sliding doors of the two patios and all the windows except those in the bedrooms located on the opposite side of Mami's room. After opening the two heavy back patio doors, I show Tío Carlos a trick to turn the key and smoothly slide the front patio, glass door. I smile with a dimple on each side of my mouth, which I got from him, and say, *"Ah, mashkut."*

The entire second floor of Casa Lau was built on top of the store and has been our home since I was about two years old. This floor is large enough to have two outdoor patios, a kitchen, a living room, a dining room, three bathrooms, five bedrooms, and a small bedroom for a maid, which Mami converted into a pantry. The house is elongated and, on the side facing *la octava*, is the kitchen with a round table and the six pink vinyl chairs where we ate all our daily meals. There is a door leading to the dining room with a rectangular long wooden table that comfortably seats ten people and where we had formal dinners to celebrate Christmas, New Year, and Chinese New Year and where we used to study and do homework with groups of young friends and classmates. We keep our two large refrigerators in the dining room, which also has a bureau that contains the chinaware we used when we had guests. This dining room faces *la octava*, where the bureau is located. On the third side are top-to-bottom windows that face a large patio where a few years later Papito hired somebody to build a fountain with an angel in the middle. The angel is holding a clay pot spouting water that fills up the fountain. We spent countless days with our neighbours and friends swimming in this shallow, 25-centimetre-deep fountain.

Between the dining room and the rest of the house is a wooden ornament case that extends from the floor to the ceiling and sits next to the window facing the patio. This case serves as a divider between the dining room and the family room areas and holds ornaments, pictures, and a swivel so we can rotate and watch TV in either side. On the living room side are two armchairs and a rocking chair facing the ornament case and the TV. There is also a sliding door to the fountain patio on one side, and on the other, a wooden door where the yellow concrete staircase descends to the gray *portón*.

Behind the TV area is a small space for Mamita's black Yamaha piano and a couple of chairs and a small round table for the telephone. The house has two wings on opposite sides: one is a long corridor that leads to three bedrooms (my parents', Vero's, and Guada's and mine) and two bathrooms; the other wing has a small hallway that leads to Mami and Teti's room, as well as to their bathroom and to Tío Juanca's room.

At the end of the house is the formal living room where we have our green-knitted top and black-vinyl bottom sofa group with a coffee table and two side tables. The sofas are in excellent shape after some thirty years of use since they have been fitted with a cloth cover that Mamita sewed and that has never been removed. The seat covers were only taken off when we had adult guests in that part of the house.

The formal living room backs into a huge sliding glass door that leads to a large half-covered patio where we used to spend most of our time playing and running and where we had birthday parties with three or four "piñatas" stuffed with candies, coins, confetti, and sometimes even flour for fun. We moved our Christmas and New Year's parties to this patio when the family became too large for the dining room; most of the bedrooms, except Vero and Tío Juanca's, also back onto it.

The back of the house is very open and faces a small valley as well as *Loma Real*, a more upscale residential neighbourhood located a few kilometres away on another hilltop and on the other side of the Cohatán River. From the formal living room, the back patio, and some of the bedrooms are uninterrupted views of blue skies during the daytime and beautiful sunsets at dusk.

As I open the sliding door, I notice that the place needs some fresh air but that it is clean. The electricity is already connected, and a truck that delivers propane will come tomorrow to fill up the close-to-empty tank on the roof of the house. I tell Tío Carlos not to worry as I still remember how to read the propane meter and how the tank works, as well as the water heaters, the stove, the water pump, and holding tanks and everything else in the house. Tía Elda has thoughtfully brought some sugar, salt, and rice from her own pantry to get us through the first few days and will take us grocery shopping before it gets too late.

I quickly turn on the faucets of the two water tanks, one next to the kitchen and the other one on the roof next to the clothesline to get some city water before it is turned off for the day (the main supply is turned on and off randomly throughout the day, so the *tanques* must be filled up if you want to keep a constant water supply). The water tanks are small, made of cement and built as part of a *lavabo,* used mostly for washing clothes. The *lavabo,* also made of stone and cement, is a horizontal long area covered with parallel ridges that go from side to side so one can scrub, stretch, turn, and hand-wash clothes. We also turn on a large water pump to fill up the main tank located behind the house. The main tank is enclosed and is the size of a large room with a ceiling higher than a person. Finally, I turn on the faucet that has a filter, from which water slowly drips out, so that when we come back, we will be able to boil water for drinking and cooking.

We then head out to a *Rialfer* to buy some food (the nearest one being *Rialfer San Juan*). The first *Rialfer (Bulevares)* opened in 1979 outside the city. Locally owned, it was basically the first supermarket chain in the area where one could buy everything needed in one spot - it had airconditioning and a parking lot. I have a certain attachment to this one located on the only boulevard of the city, where we used to go for a spin and kill time. In this *Rialfer*, we got to know what slurpees and soft ice cream cones were, and we also got our only studio family portrait taken, which sits on the mantle in the house of my parents, who currently live in Vancouver, Canada, just as I do.

After shopping, it is quite late so Tío and Tía drop us off. And while Mami puts away the things we bought, I sweep and mop and put some mismatched sheets on one of the three beds in Mami's room. Mami is going to sleep on her old mattress-less hard bed, which she has had for as long as I can remember. I remind her that the day is over and that she needs to be in bed by 9:00 p.m. or as she says, "My time to fall asleep expires." And since she wakes up around 5:00 a.m., she will not be able to get any rest if she does not go to sleep soon.

I am completely exhausted, so I instinctively go around closing and locking all of the doors as well as turning off all the faucets that fill up the *tanques* in case the city water is suddenly turned on in the middle of the night. Before going to sleep, Mami puts a blanket beside me and reminds me that I will need one in the middle of the night. I nod in agreement and accept the blanket, then turn off the bedroom light and say, "*Chou tau*, Mami" ("Get some rest soon, Mami"). I leave the door ajar so the bathroom light shines through and it is not so dark for Mami when she wakes up in the middle of the night.

Around 3:00 a.m. I wake up looking for the blanket (Mami is right – it is cold). Once I am covered up, I feel peaceful and can only hear a rooster somewhere in the distance and the whistle of the *velador* doing his security rounds in the neighbourhood.

Then I fall fast asleep again.

4

MAMI'S
WEDDING DAY

MAMI as usual gets up at 5:00 a.m. and goes straight to what she calls *mi oficina* (the kitchen) to boil filtered water, wash all the necessary dishes and pots, and set up the kitchen the way she likes it. Then, she goes around inspecting the dry goods she had left the last time she was here: grains and cookies and crackers and cans of food. She does not look at expiry dates but instead smells and looks for signs of mould and staleness as well as brown liquids oozing from any bulging cans. And since she finds nothing of the sort, in spite the fact that at least three years have gone by, she happily places these items on the counter so we can have them throughout our stay.

I get up at 6:30 a.m. and soon hear somebody yelling *"el gas."* So I quickly put on shorts and a cotton blouse and run to the roof to meet the propane delivery person. Once there, I notice a young, dark-skinned man hooking up a long hose that reaches from the service truck parked two stories below to our propane tank. After the tank is filled, he gives me an invoice and then very adeptly climbs back down the truck ladder. Next, I join Mami in the execution of a few house chores like cleaning the bathroom and lighting the water heater that will be needed for the bathroom we will be using.

Mami has already gone to briefly visit Tía Nelly and Ka-Yeh, both of whom I address as *Kei-Ma* and *Ka-Yeh*, or godparents, when speaking in Chinese but as "aunt" and "godfather" when speaking in Spanish. They used to own *el Gigante,* a grocery store, on one of the other three corners opposite Casa Lau. But in the late 1970s or early 1980s, they opened up a very successful Chinese restaurant barely half a block away called *Kam Long.* During her visit, Mami puts in a request for Chinese vegetables, seafood, and chicken for Tía Nelly to pick up when she goes to the market to do the shopping for the restaurant. When Casa Lau was open, Ka-Yeh used to come by every late afternoon near closing time (when both businesses were relatively quiet) to chat. Since Ka-Yeh is also from Kau Kong, in southern China, as are Teti and Papito, they would get into discussions about everything in *Kau Kong Wah.* Later when Teti was not around, the discussions continued with Papito and sometimes Mamita joining in.

After cleaning up, Mami and I sit at the round kitchen table on two of the pink vinyl chairs that are part of the set my father, Papito, had bought perhaps more than thirty years ago after one of the walls was knocked down to make room for an open-style kitchen. The kitchen has wood cabinets and windows with bars just like any window or sliding glass door that faces a bustling, major street below, like *la octava norte* (North 8th Avenue). On the other side, there is a green iron staircase that leads to the *azotea*, an open rooftop deck where we have a second *lavadero* made of cement for washing clothes by hand and a few clotheslines. The kitchen has a large gas cooking stove, and beside it there is a light blue-tiled, gas structure that resembles an outdoor barbecue pit, only it has a hole on top big enough to place a large *wok*. This is what Mami prefers to use when cooking and had requested to be put it in when the kitchen was built.

Since only Mami and I are in the house right now, I am thinking that this would be a perfect opportunity to get more of an understanding of our shared past. There used to be so much activity in this kitchen with so many of us living here. Come to think of it, it was never the custom for us to talk at home. During meals, adults would converse briefly while we children were to keep quiet and concentrate on our food and on showing good manners. Children could not intervene or ask questions when adults were discussing adult topics. So anything that was discussed never seemed interesting to me at all. Most of the time adults talked about what was going on or affected them at the time: family affairs, problems at the store, the neighbours, news in the community. In general, meals were quiet, and any comments that came up were basically about the meal we were having or planning to have.

So I ask Mami to tell me about her wedding day.

"When I got married, it was a special and BIG celebration. We had a pond of gold fish made up, and there was loud music and lots of food. It was so lively!! Usually the bride's family gives money like a dowry, and the bride's mother uses it to buy all the basic furniture needed. In my case, my mother used the dowry money to buy a living room set and a bedroom set. Very often the bride's relatives have to put in extra money to buy these essentials. The bride's family is also in charge of the food for the actual ceremony as well as for feeding the people who help to build the house for the newlyweds and those who help to move the furniture in."

"The groom's family has it easy as they don't have to do anything except just give some money and be in charge of the tea ceremony. This takes place in the groom's home. Both families gather and sit in a row starting in the middle with the parents of the groom and bride, then moving outwards with the rest of the family members seated by hierarchy (the older one is, the higher one is considered). The bride serves tea to her in-laws first; then both the bride and the groom serve tea to the bride's parents and then to everybody else going also by hierarchy. The groom's parents and all their close relatives give the bride jewelry, and it is best if the jewelry is made of gold. It sounds complicated, don't you think? I am not even sure I remember everything that well; it was so long ago."

Mami stops, reflects a bit and adds, "On the wedding day, you stay with your in-laws, and you are not allowed to visit your parents' house until after the third day. These are our customs in Kau Kong. We have so many different traditions that are strange and interesting at the same time. And they are different from here to the next town which could be just there," she says pointing only a few metres away. "And maybe the new generations don't even follow these customs," she adds with a bit of wonder and disappointment.

Hesitantly she finally adds, "I was a very lucky woman. I had never met or knew anything or had seen your grandfather before the day we got married. I just did what I was told and married him. I don't even know how old he was, but he was a much older man. Calculating your dad's age, I'd say I was more or less nineteen years old when I got married, and Teti must have been around thirty-five or thirty-six."

"I really cared for and loved Teti very much. He always took very good care of me. He gave me a home, food, children, and I never lacked anything. And he never hit me or treated me disrespectfully. I can tell you that many women did not have the same luck. Their husbands would treat them very badly, and the wives had to stay with them and take the abuse. There was no such thing as a divorce or separation. You couldn't choose your husband and you married for life. There were a lot of mistreated women, and I was not at all. I was one of the lucky few." She says this with a smile and with some tears in her eyes.

"My mother told me later that there were many men returning to China who wanted to marry me. In fact, there had been a Chinese man who had returned from Huixtla [very near Tapachula] who had seen me and fallen in love. He was young and very persuasive, but my mother did not think he had good manners or knew proper etiquette; so he was never approved of. My mother said that when he came to visit my parents, he sat with his legs open and all over the place. My mom did not like this at all; it was not a good sign. So he was not even a candidate for me."

Before Mami has a chance to tell me any more, Tío Carlos and Tía Elda come over to pick us up. From Mami's constant complaints, they know that there are no Chinese restaurants in Campeche City. So they want to take her to one of the well-established local *tapachulteco* Chinese restaurants for the customary Sunday family lunch. Tío honks his car horn and Tía Elda gets out of the car to ring our doorbell, which is not sounding that clearly because of the rust. After locking the wooden door, Mami and I go down the yellow staircase, and we all greet each other with a kiss on the right cheek.

We purposely head out one hour earlier than our reservation in order to make a planned visit to my Grandpa Teti at the cemetery. Teti, Tío Pepe, and my sister Angelita's graves are housed in a small cement chapel in the *Panteón Jardínes*. Almost every Sunday, Mami and I used to take flowers and clean their graves as well as the inside and outside of the chapel. After, we would stop by a tombstone located a few spots over and behind to light a candle. Written in Chinese on a free-standing simple gravestone is the name of Mami's nephew, Ramón's.

This visit is no different. After inspecting the outside, I unlock the metal door of the chapel and, together with Tío Carlos and Tía Elda, brush away the dust and sprinkle water around all the graves, but instead of flowers we light lots of candles in glass containers. While we are cleaning, Tía Elda points out that my uncle, Tío Neto (Tío Carlos' older brother), has had someone put a fresh coat of white paint on the chapel. She adds that in the absence of Mami's weekly visits, Tío Neto has been the one coming diligently in all these years to look after Teti. Mami nods, feeling very grateful.

Tío Carlos and Tía Elda head back to retrieve the car, giving Mami and me a little time alone in the cemetery. In front of Teti's gravestone, Mami clasps her hands together close to her chest and slowly shakes them back and forth three times, paying her respects to her husband. Then, I hold her arm and we stand for a minute with tears in our eyes until the voices somewhere in the distance bring us back to reality. I put away the candles, the brush, the broom, and the bucket and lock the door of the chapel. Afterwards we head to Ramón's grave, located a row behind the chapel where Teti rests. We take away all the weeds, clean the site, and light a candle. Finally, in silence, we walk out of the cemetery to where Tío Carlos and Tía Elda are waiting for us.

We get into the car and with windows down head to the restaurant. On our way, we drive past familiar sites like *Hotel Kamico* where our family used to eat Sunday brunch and where Don Miguel, the German general manager at the time, gave us permission to swim in the hotel's "guests-only" pool. Then, we pass by *la Quinta Carmelita*, a typical family restaurant where they used to serve the best *pozole* soup and the most delicious *champurrado* (a hot thick sweetened drink made of maize). We also drive by *el Colegio Miguel Hidalgo* (where my sister Guada and I went to high school) and pass by houses where I remember visiting friends.

Then we take a brief tour of a few downtown spots like the *Parque Central*, the church, and city hall before we head to *el Mandarín* just a few blocks away from the centre of town. As we drive past the *Iglesia de San Agustín*, the well-visited church located in front of the main park, I catch myself instinctively drawing a cross in the air with my right hand as I always did when passing by any church in Mexico while growing up. I notice Mami and Tía Elda automatically doing the same thing, taking their right thumb and index finger together to make a vertical line starting from their foreheads to their chests and ending with a horizontal line from their left shoulders to their right ones. Suddenly I realize how natural this gesture seems here, but how odd that I never make it when I pass by a church anywhere else in the world.

We arrive at *el Mandarín* and park on the restaurant's gravel parking lot located across the street. As we get out, Tía Elda manages to pluck five bright green, ripe limes hanging from a lush, enormous tree standing in the middle of the lot providing shade to the parked cars. I remember when I used to go down to the lower patio near the main water tank behind the house to our lime tree. I would take along one of the long sticks used in the store to lower products that were placed on the top shelves and cut down a bucket of limes every time Mami ran out of them.

From the lot, we cross the street and head towards the house entrance where the owners have lived since as long as I can remember. We walk in unannounced through the hallway and pass a bedroom ending up in the kitchen to say hello to Doña Lidia, who is busy making sure every dish is cooked, seasoned, and arranged properly. I am so glad to see her and my heart feels so at ease when we hug each other with the same familiarity as if we have not missed a day. She has been one of Mamita's few close friends and a trained nurse, so all of us would come to her house to get shots when we were sick.

We then head to the service door that leads into the restaurant and stop by the cashier where Don Manuel is sitting with a smile, welcoming customers and ensuring that everyone is being looked after. Don Manuel and Doña Lidia have three sons around my age; so I used to play with them at the beach. We went to the same high school and had even been in the same English classes in the afternoons at *la UNACH*. When we were younger, Don Manuel owned a lot on the beach near Tapachula, so almost every Sunday a large group of Chinese families used to gather to swim, play *mah-jong*, eat, and chat.

Since Casa Lau, like all the other Chinese-owned retail stores, was open on Sundays until 2:00 p.m., Don Manuel would come by in his truck and pick us kids up around 7:00 a.m. Later in the day after closing the clothing stores, the fabric stores, and the grocery stores, the grown-ups would show up and spend the rest of the day relaxing on the beach. Deep-fried soy sauce chicken and orange-flavoured sponge cake were always must-haves during these outings.

We all sit down in the airconditioned restaurant to enjoy the food. Tío Carlos and Tía Elda have pre-ordered some fancy dishes to welcome us home. In between orders, Don Manuel and Doña Lidia escape from their duties and take turns to sit and chat with us. Their granddaughters and daughter-in-law drop by the restaurant and join us briefly for a snack. After a lot of catching up, reminiscing, and laughs, we say goodbye, and Tío Carlos and Tía Elda drive Mami and me home while the ominous clouds and lightning and thunder perform a spectacular show.

As another hot and humid day in Tapachula draws to a close, I reflect on the coldness of Vancouver and think, *this is heaven*. November is not considered part of the rainy season, but the torrential rains are here, just like in September and October when it pours for three hours in the late afternoon and the streets become rivers.

5

AS THE WAR BEGINS...

TODAY is very sunny and the only trace of the passing storm is the smell of yesterday's rain. A smell that reminds me of my childhood years spent in this house where the tastes of rain, jungle, humidity, and the salty sea are combined with the aromas of Mexican spices and Chinese food.

Weather has never been a subject of discussion in this part of the world because it is usually not so hot, hot, or extremely hot throughout the year. The only difference is that during the rainy season the sky, like clockwork, turns dark and is filled with moisture-saturated clouds, and for three to four hours in the afternoon huge drops that look more like curtains of rain fall incessantly.

Mami has just poured a large portion of oatmeal into a big Chinese bowl and is ordering me to finish and not leave any leftovers. The potful she has made would feed at least three people. At the same time she is telling me to be hungry for lunch as she will be buying freshly made *tortillas* and making something she insists we do not have and cannot find in Vancouver (or in Canada for that matter) - some *camarones gigantes a la plancha* (pan-fried giant prawns). I gather that Tía Nelly went to the market this morning and asked one of her helpers to drop off Mami's shopping requests.

After getting up at 5:00 a.m. again, Mami resumed her daily exercise routine, which entails walking around in circles ten times on one of the patios. Life in Tapachula starts early compared to in Vancouver. By 5:00 a.m., one of the local *mercados* is bustling with merchants selling vegetables, fruits, spices, blankets, candies, grains, breads, tortillas, tin goods, plastic household items, and local crafts. Food stands are already serving cold *choco milk* and freshly deep-fried *churros*, as well as a wide variety of Mexican *antojitos* and even Chinese food.

The *finqueros* as well as the native Indian groups like the Chamulas and the Zapotecas have come from nearby *ejidos* and down from the mountains to buy supplies. Housewives and maids have joined in the wheeling and dealing of price-bargaining for fresh ingredients to be used in that day's cooking.

Inside Casa Lau it is now 10:30 a.m. and Mami has just finished cooking our second meal of the day: sunny-side-up eggs, tortillas, salsa, and black bean soup. Having had a hearty bowl of oatmeal barely four hours ago, I am not sure where in my stomach I will be able to find an empty spot. When Casa Lau was still in business, breakfast of coffee and sweet bread would be served at 6:30 a.m., with family lunch at 2:00 p.m. But Mami would prepare a second meal at 10:00 a.m. consisting of leftovers or fried eggs, rice, and soup for Teti and my parents, who would take turns coming upstairs from the store to eat. Now that we have returned to Casa Lau, for some reason Mami has reverted to this old custom regardless of what she does in Campeche or I do in Vancouver. All I know is that Mami will expect to see an empty plate by the end of the meal; so it is better that I forget about thinking and concentrate on eating.

"*¿Qué ma' quele come?*" ("What else would you like to eat?"), Mami asks.

I look at her with eyes wide open and respond in Chinese, "Mami, there is a lot of food here that I don't think I will be able to finish."

"No, what else would you like to have while you are here that you cannot eat in Canada? When you were little, I had to buy you *churros* or *nuegados* on Sunday mornings on our way back from the market so you would go with me. So how about some *churros*?"

Almost every Sunday, Mami went to church at 4:00 a.m. and then to the market for fresh vegetables and fruits. She used to bribe one of us girls to go with her and help her carry one of the baskets in exchange for a bag of deep-fried sweet pastries. Most often, I was the one who ended up going with her. Guada, my older sister, always had a hard time leaving her bed, and Mami's impatience to start her day could not wait for Guada's constant *dáme cinco minutitos más* ("Give me five more minutes") or *despiértame en diez minutos* ("Wake me up again in ten") every time she was woken up. Vero, my youngest sister, was always considered the baby of the family and therefore was rarely asked to get up so early.

"*Churros* would be great!!" I respond.

Mami smiles broadly and sits down with chopsticks in her hand and starts breaking away the fried eggs. Then she puts her chopsticks on the side of her plate and breaks her tortilla in half, places one half on her plate and again picks up her chopsticks. She holds the other half of the tortilla in her left hand while she stuffs it with a piece of egg, black beans, and salsa using chopsticks in her right hand. Then she puts the taco in her mouth. She continues scooping everything - eggs, beans, and salsa - using her tortilla and chopsticks until she finishes her food.

I ask Mami if she remembers what happened when the war started. She looks at me and says, "Such a difficult time; so long ago," and then she continues.

"Around 1935, we got married and for about a year and a half, we lived together in an old house Teti had managed to purchase with some money he had brought from Mexico. I got pregnant and Papito was born in 1937 just as Teti received an urgent letter from Sr. Paco Isasi, one of his close friends, who sent money for the boat trip back to Tapachula. Casa Lau was quickly disappearing because Gustavo, a nephew

Teti had sponsored from Kau Kong, was gambling the entire merchandise away and the building would be next. With this news and the war approaching, Teti headed to Hong Kong."

"The war was already underway in China, and Kau Kong had become increasingly unsafe and a target. You could already hear shooting and bombs being dropped, and by this time, my father and most of my brothers and my brothers' families as well as most of Teti's relatives had left Kau Kong. Some headed for the safety of Hong Kong, and some of my brothers ran and remained hidden in other parts in China. Two of my brothers went to Hoi Lam in the middle of Vietnam, and another one made it all the way into South Vietnam."

"Shortly after Teti left, my brother #13 took me and your father, Papito, to Hong Kong. One night during our boat trip, we were trying to be very quiet so we wouldn't get caught by the Japanese. Your father's tummy was hurting and he wouldn't stop crying. I got some cooking oil and rubbed his tummy, but whenever I stopped, he would cry in pain. Suddenly, everyone in the small boat was whispering and demanding me to throw him overboard, otherwise we would all get caught. But how could I do that? He was only a baby, and I was wishing my mother-in-law were there to put some herbs together to cover his tummy. But she wasn't so I just kept rubbing his tummy until he fell asleep. Everyone was so mad at me, but I would have never done any harm to my child."

Mami meets her brother #14 for the first time
in more than 20 years in San Francisco. Here
enjoying dinner with their sister #11 (mid 1970s).

Tïa Chusita and Mami visiting Mami's sister #11
(on the right) in San Francisco (mid 1970s).

"Twelve days later, my mother, Teti's mother, Teti's eldest sister, and some cousins from Teti's side left Kau Kong to join us in Hong Kong. So I decided to divide our already tiny room in Hong Kong into four even smaller rooms. Meanwhile, Teti was waiting for a spot on a boat that would take him back to Mexico on a forty-day journey. While in Hong Kong, he was staying with one of his uncles who owned a store and would meet up with us at night. Papito was not even one year old when Teti left for Mexico, and I was left in Hong Kong in charge of the family comprised of Papito, my mother-in-law, and Teti's elder sister, Tai-Ku, who was my sister-in-law #2."

"Before Teti arrived in Mexico, my father passed away in Hong Kong from tetanus (a virus got into his brain from an open wound due to a fall while going to the market with one of his grandchildren). We kept my father's body in our room until we buried him. Then we moved to my father's room where I shared a small bed with your Dad and Tai-Ku. My mother-in-law slept on a wooden board next to us."

"Three months after Teti left Hong Kong, I received news from Tapachula that the store had been emptied, the merchandise just gambled away by his nephew. To avoid completely losing the building, Teti would wrap stones and bricks with newspapers and place them all over the shelves so it would look like the store was full of merchandise and open for business. In the meanwhile, he was asking around among his friends to borrow some more merchandise and money. He knew it was going to take him a long time to get back on his feet but did not want to worry me, so he tried to sound cheerful and optimistic. But I still felt it was a painful letter and hard times were coming our way."

Mami shifts uncomfortably in her chair, a sign for me to start picking up the dishes and put them in the sink. At that very moment, I recall my mother, Mamita's, daily exhortation to me and my sisters, "Okay you know whose turn it is to wash and who is in charge of rinsing and who will dry..." before leaving the kitchen. There were three of us and three chores which we rotated every day after lunch and dinner. We all liked to wash or rinse, but we all hated to dry since that entailed also putting dishes neatly away. This time, however, it is only me, and I do the chores of washing and rinsing happily because I welcome any form of exercise that will get me moving and hopefully make some room for more food later on. Besides, Mami has asked me to let the dishes dry by themselves since we have more than enough for the two of us.

Mami spreads a bunch of dry black beans on the table and cleans them by picking out all the twigs as well as dirt, sand, grains, and small pebbles that could break a tooth. She is quite adept and quickly starts forming two piles: one that has nothing but black beans and a second one with all the unwanted extras. She is talking in a quite lively way and telling me she will do the same thing with rice, pointing at a rusty tin container that was bought at least twenty-five years ago and used to hold Cal-C-Tose (a chocolate-flavoured nutritional powder to add to milk). Just like this tin, every container and glass jar in almost every household I ever visited when I was growing up has been cleaned and re-used to store goods. I think the only plastic Tupperware I ever used and saw was at school to bring sandwiches for recess, and even then it was considered a luxury.

I am brought back to the present by Mami's continuous complaints about dry beans and rice not sold already cleaned here in Mexico. She finally says, "I bet you don't have to do all this in Canada. The beans and the rice must already come clean over there, just like everything else. That's good. You're lucky."

6

STAYING ALIVE

IT is 1:30 p.m. The sky is blue, the sun is right on top of our heads, and the heat is intense. Mami and I are slowly making our way back home, and the streets are full of energy. Uniformed kids are finishing school and rushing to go home; young girls are being sent to the nearest *tortillería* to buy the freshest corn tortillas with a colourful and clean *manta* in hand that is used to wrap and keep this main staple warm; shops are getting ready to close; everyone is scurrying home to eat lunch, the largest meal of the day, with their families. Like clockwork, at 2:00 p.m. the streets become quiet and deserted, and the only sound I can hear from afar is of a metal curtain being pulled down as the last shop closes.

At the sight of those children, I try to guess what school they attend by the uniform they wear. The colours are different from what I remember, but the patterns are still the same. There are many more schools now, so I am having a hard time guessing correctly. Mami tells me that even when her own children were going to school, it was impossible for her to match schools and uniforms.

In my time, there were fewer schools, so it was easier to determine what school someone attended as well as what grade just by looking at the uniform. Public schools had better teachers and won most scholastic competitions at both the city and state levels. So my parents decided that all three girls would attend public schools for the first nine years. For the six years I attended *la Tipo Fronteriza* elementary school, I wore a red overall skirt, white blouse, black shoes, and white socks. For secondary or middle school, I went to *la Federal Uno* and wore a sleeveless dress, which was pink in first grade, blue in second, and wine red in third (accompanied as usual by a white blouse, black shoes, and white socks). In high school, *el Colegio Miguel Hidalgo* (a private Catholic school), I wore a finely-chequered gray skirt and white blouse. At that time, the only alternative was *la Prepa Uno*, a public school that closed down too often because of teachers' strikes that caused students to miss a grade. Regardless of the grade or school, everyone's uniforms had to fit properly, and be spotless and wrinkle-free, no buttons or zippers missing and shoes always polished.

Mami and I are slowly making our way back home from the closest *tortillería*. Earlier, Mami decided that we had to have freshly-made tortillas since I cannot get these in Canada. So with a clean piece of *manta*, we walked down the street and joined the line-up of young girls. As the machine spits out the tortillas, the smell is too much to resist. So as soon as we pay a few pesos for our half kilo, I open up the corners of our *manta*, roll up a piping hot tortilla and devour it. Mami smiles and says, "You see? I knew this was a good idea."

Mami and I sit at the kitchen table where a mountain of gigantic prawns lays beside the pile of tortillas we just bought. In between these two dishes is a small plate where I have mixed *catsup* (ketchup) and mayo to make the customary *salsa rusa* dressing to accompany the prawns. Mami has a bowl of rice in front of her and tells me she only made enough rice for her because I should reserve space in my stomach for more prawns and avoid getting full with rice.

"*Sek fan*, Mami" ("Eat rice, Mami"), I say in Chinese the customary address and I serve her the biggest prawn I can see.

She starts complaining, reverses her chopsticks, and serves me an even larger one that she has managed to pull out of the pile of gigantic prawns. Then she reverses back her chopsticks and with a smile says, "Don't serve me. You are the guest."

I see her, from the corner of my eye, take her bowl in her left hand and chopsticks in her right hand, then place the bowl on her lips and adeptly and quickly push rice into her mouth with her chopsticks, all in one automatic and natural motion. Then I begin eating as well.

At that moment, I recall the look of disbelief in Coly (one of my two Mexican friends), who had been allowed to join us for lunch one afternoon when I was a little girl. I could see her mouth drop open as her big curious eyes watched us all eat with chopsticks and bowls instead of plates and forks. She looked quite stunned trying to follow our table rituals and manners, which were so different from what she was used to in her home. The following day, and contrary to what I expected, she came up to me and said her parents (both well-known teachers) had given her permission to play and stay for lunch at our home any time and that I was also welcome to come and eat at her house as well. Coly then became my first best friend in first grade outside of the Chinese community.

I look at Mami, as we savour our last prawns, and she frowns, pointing out that to reheat them will make the meat very tough and fishy, so we cannot have leftovers. "Tell me the rest of the story about what happened to you during the war when Teti left you in Hong Kong."

"I lived there for close to three years. Life was tough as living conditions were tight, but it still seemed uneventful. I did not have to work and there was food. Teti would send us a bit of money from Mexico once in a while. We had to be quite thrifty, but other than that, things were not so bad."

"However, things became quite difficult when the Japanese attacked Pearl Harbor and shortly after Hong Kong in late 1941. I took my mother-in-law, sister-in-law, Tai-Ku, and Papito to Macau (sixty kilometres west of Hong Kong). My *Ah-Yeh* (paternal grandfather) had an acquaintance there who had a store where he sold soybean products (such as fermented bean sauce and black bean sauce). We took a *lancha* (a small boat more like a canoe) from Hong Kong to Macau, being careful not to be in the open for too long."

"Teti was able to send money to the store several times, and I could receive it until the Japanese got too close. Then we ran to places of refuge where we knew somebody with a store so I could get letters and money from Teti. But rent was expensive in Macau, so we decided to live in Tam Chai (in the outskirts, twenty kilometres away) where my mother and some of her brothers' wives already were. From there I would head back to Macau to look for work and to check every now and then for news from Mexico."

It was around this time that everything became one long movie scene in Mami's head with days, nights, months, and years becoming a blur between running and surviving, between life and death.

Shops closed down as people feared for their lives and ran away to avoid the Japanese; there were no jobs; food became very scarce; people were dying everywhere. Mami's godson, her youngest great-uncle, and the wife of Mami's brother #11 died in Tam Chai during this time either because of starvation or disease. Mami managed to get a government job carrying buckets of sand and soil for the trenches.

"Tai-Ku would take care of your Dad, so I started work very early and finished around 4:00 in the afternoon. It was a slow and tiring process. I would climb up a steep hill, fill up the buckets with sand and soil, carry them down and dump them in the trenches all day long. The good thing is that I earned about a pound of rice a day that I could take home and we would mix it with wild yams and yucca. After our shift on Saturdays, we would get about half a pound extra for Sundays, our day of rest. I also got a bowl of thick rice congee for lunch, so I would have a full stomach almost every day. Getting rice was good because money would not have gotten us anything since all the shops were closed down. And with this rice I could feed my mother-in-law, Tai-Ku, and your father."

Mami, her mother-in-law, sister-in-law Tai-Ku, and Papito stayed around Macau and Tam Chai for a few years. Then they were forced to move around to stay alive. Mami remembers this time of constant moving and running, starting at dawn and ending at dusk, day after day. From Tam Chai they headed north to Kong Chau then back to Kau Kong, where they were able to pass by her father's house briefly. Then Mami decided that it would be safer to move north again into the countryside to small places like Sah-Peng, Lok-Tong, Yeung-Mui, and Pak-Tou, until they reached Kong-Sei. Mami was young and walked while two men, whom Mami had hired, carried her mother-in-law and Tai-Ku with Papito sitting on her lap. They both sat on two hard, uncomfortable wooden chairs tied to two posts, which the hired men carried.

There was no room to take anything but a few pieces of clothing and blankets with a few pieces of jewelry cleverly sewn inside. Their days would end when they could not stand up anymore, falling down from hunger and exhaustion with their feet covered in bruises and open wounds. This was the only and the fastest way that they could outrun the Japanese.

In Kong-Sei, Mami waited for news and money from Teti. Ah-Lau San, one of Teti's friends in Tapachula, who sold candles just half a block away from him, had a son-in-law who had a store in Kong-Sei. This way Teti was able to send money through Ah-Lau San in Tapachula to the business in Kong-Sei and eventually to Mami. But just like in other places before, whenever they received money, some relative or friend would ask for a loan, and Mami never had the heart to say "no." So part of the funds she received in Kong-Sei was shared with others. After receiving money a few times, the three women and the small boy headed to Heong-Ha and then to Ng-Chau where they looked for a man who also had the last name of Lau. They found him and his wife who let them live with them briefly. This allowed Papito, who was about six years old, to begin his first schooling. It was not anything formal, but he sat on a stool and had his first lessons at a teacher's house. This was short-lived, however, because they had to run again to Tai-Lok.

Everywhere they went, the people they encountered

advised Mami to sell Papito. One could get good money, so desperately needed in those difficult times, by selling one's son. This would also have allowed Mami, her mother-in-law, and Tai-Ku more mobility and more food per person. As for the child, he would most likely be taken into a wealthier family where he would get proper food and better living conditions. People even suggested to Mami to ask Tai-Ku to sell Papito if Mami did not have the heart to do it.

"But I thought, then why would I want to run? What would be my purpose in life? There was no purpose without my son. So I kept your Dad and selfishly thought that at the end, it just would be better to die together when the time came than to be apart for the rest of our lives."

"This time in Tai-Lok was the most difficult we had to face. I could not receive any communication from Teti, so we weren't able to get any money from him or receive any news. I had to work every day, all day long carrying buckets of water back and forth from a river and only earned about five coins per bucket. I had to strap one bucket on each side of a stick and carry the stick on my shoulders so that I could get ten coins for each trip. But there was no rice anymore and no lunches at work either. My body ached all the time and I no longer had shoes."

"Tai-Ku was left in charge of the household. She took care of her own mother and of Papito and cooked whatever plants and bulbs I was able to bring home for dinner. But one day while I was away working, my mother-in-law passed away. That was terrible because I didn't see my mother-in-law when she was dying. And then, we didn't have money for a proper burial. We just put some planks of wood together and placed her there and nothing else. We prayed for forgiveness and tried to convince ourselves that my mother-in-law's soul and Teti would have understood under the circumstances. Then Tai-Ku went to the market to sell the few possessions her mother had on her so that we could pay for the rent."

After Mami's mother-in-law's death, they consoled themselves by thinking that at least there was one less person to feed. But to make matters worse, Papito got painful stomachaches, and Tai-Ku had to search for a doctor. Papito, like everyone else, was simply not receiving proper nutrition and got sick recurrently. Other than boiled grass and wild yams and the occasional rice, they ate home-made *min-si* (preserved soybean sauce). Less often, they bought salted fish or salted vegetables but only if they could find them and had the extra coins to spare. There were no fresh vegetables or meats or fish anywhere to be found.

"Sometimes we made *min-si* with dry soybeans we bought, cooking them for a long time. Then we let them sit until the beans got fermented and then added salt. Finally, we took the fermented beans out in the sun to dry. It tasted okay on top of steamed rice, and it was quite nutritious. But we had to continue eating what we found in the fields to survive."

"One day I came in from work dragging my feet, completely exhausted and right there at the door your Dad, who was six years old, received me all excitedly. It was suppertime and Tai-Ku had taught him how to make rice. So he grabbed my hand and very innocently said to me, 'Food is ready. I made supper for you tonight. From now on, I can be in charge of food so when you come home we can all eat and you can rest. Aren't you proud of me?' It was indeed my proudest moment."

Gold was their salvation during these tough times. One by one Mami sold the few pieces of gold jewelry she had been given for her wedding. Gold was worth quite a bit, and the few basic things they needed were not expensive. So by selling a chain or a necklace here and there, they had enough money to last them for a while. Now I understand why Mami and Teti sometimes gave us gold or silver coins on birthdays. They wanted us to have something of value in case we were ever in a difficult situation and needed them for our own survival; they were making sure we had "insurance."

"Tai-Ku, Papito, and I were able to remain hidden in the countryside for a while until news arrived that the war was over. At first I was not totally sure and I did not want to risk our lives. So we waited a few more days until I could not hear any more bombs or shots and felt that the Japanese were really gone. Once we heard that peace had returned to the cities, we headed to Kong Chau looking for Ah-Bun, one of Teti's nieces, who owned a tailor shop with her husband. They worked together sewing and stitching all sorts of clothing in the shop."

"Once again I asked Tai-Ku to care for Papito, who had turned eight at the time, so that I could be mobile and get a well-paying job. Ah-Bun was totally against this idea and convinced me to stay in charge of all household chores in exchange for free room and board. But it was no vacation."

"I started early every day fetching water for the house, washing clothes, cooking all the meals, cleaning, and then in the late afternoon I helped out in the small, but busy shop sewing and mending people's clothes until the evening time when my eyes watered and I could not see clearly anymore. At nighttime, I shared a small bed with Tai-Ku and Papito in one corner of the shop. We stayed put at Ah-Bun's until we reconnected with Teti."

On the other side of the globe, Teti was greatly relieved to learn that his family had survived the war. He sent Mami money which took about four weeks to arrive but allowed her, Tai-Ku, and Papito to rent an apartment about a block away from the shop. There was also enough money for Mami to buy food supplies to thank Ah-Bun, who did not want to take any money from them. With more stability and more financial security, Papito (who was nearly nine by then) resumed school without any further interruptions. And at last, the war was finally over for Mami and her family.

7

EATING
AND COOKING

THIS morning Mami is cooking some *plátanos machos* or plantains in water, sugar, and cinnamon sticks for breakfast. I take two pieces out of the pot, remove the peels, and mash the plantains. On the table, there is already a piece of fresh, salty, crumbly cheese nicely wrapped in a green banana leaf and a plastic bag of fresh, thick cream. Mami looks over and smiles at me.

"At 6:00 a.m., while doing my daily exercise routine in the front patio, I heard the voice of the woman selling cheeses and cream from the street below. I was on my last round around the patio. I leaned over the railing and asked her to come to our silver *portón* so I could buy a piece of cheese and a bag of cream. Everything was so fresh so it was difficult to choose."

While I listen to Mami recount this, I put crumbled chunks of cheese on my mashed plantains and pour some cream on top of them. I try to ignore all the calories and focus instead on enjoying this delicious dish. But Mami is already talking about making some type of Mexican-style beef and fish soup for lunch.

After breakfast, I head to Papito's bedroom to look for a TV for Mami who is afraid of missing any part of the soap opera she has been following so diligently for the last few months. She mentions the title and gives me a brief description of the story line. I have no interest but try to listen to Mami so I do not disappoint her. I quickly realize that Mexican soaps have not changed one bit: young, poor, uneducated woman from a small town comes to the big city in search of a better life. She falls in love with a rich and powerful man. But it can never be since his family opposes this union as both woman and man come from two different socioeconomic levels of society. After many struggles, they finally get married and live happily ever after. The end.

Listening to Mami speak with so much enthusiasm about her soap, I hurry to find Papito's TV. When we were growing up my parents' room was off-limits, and nobody, with the exception of my youngest sister Vero, was allowed in it. Being the baby in the family, Vero would stay to explore my parents' closets and would secretly bring out candies and cookies my parents had bought in Guatemala. Though neither my mother, Mamita, nor my father, Papito, is here this time, I feel as if I am entering prohibited territory and should be brief in my search for the TV. Luckily, I find an old one with dials (though without a remote control), and Mami is quite happy because her soap is broadcast on an antenna-accessible channel.

I leave Mami with the TV and decide to return to Papito's room. I cannot resist the opportunity to go over all the closets and bureaus. I am enjoying this so much that I cannot stop myself and continue my search for hidden treasures in the rest of the house, just as I loved doing when I was little. I carefully take my time, looking into every piece of furniture and every corner in all the rooms. But what strikes me the most is that all the wooden bedframes (with their beautiful headboards), side tables, desks, and chairs and floor-to-ceiling closets were made to order so that they would fit and properly fill each bedroom. And in spite of the years, sun, and moisture they are all still in excellent condition.

However, most items that have sentimental value for me are gone. What is left are Papito's Chinese books, entire collections of old issues of *National Geographic* and *Reader's Digest* in both English and Spanish. Still, I enjoy the sensation of being surrounded by a dusty familiar surrounding and a memorable space.

I see Mami is finished testing the TV to make sure it works later when her soap is on and is also finished preparing lunch. So she joins me to inspect her bedroom, where we are surprised to discover all of her and Teti's old photo albums. We carefully turn each page and look at the pictures while Mami explains who each unfamiliar face is.

"These are very old pictures." She laughs. "Here we

are in China with your uncles and aunts when they were small. This is when we went to Guatemala, I think. This is a nephew who I know has passed away. And these are people you have never met, and I don't think you ever will. No point in remembering who's who... Oh, I don't have pictures of when I was growing up. It was not common to take photos like now, when everybody takes pictures for everything. I don't remember even seeing a camera so I don't know how to use one."

Mami looks at me and very decisively tells me, "You can have everything in my closet and in Teti's working desk to take back to Canada. The albums are getting dusty and the pictures are getting eaten by termites. And nobody looks at them anyways, so it's better that you keep them."

I smile with a big thank you and respond that I would love to take all the albums with me. And after we finish looking at the photos, I carefully place these important and cherished memorabilia in a plastic bag and put them into the most protected corner of my suitcase. Then I head to Mami's *oficina* and set the table.

There is a mountain of *milanesas*, thinly sliced breaded pieces of beef, next to a plate of *mayonesa* (mayonnaise) and limes on the table. "A kilo of beef *filete* is very expensive," Mami says, "but since this is a special occasion and I don't use my money for anything else but to buy food, we're allowed to splurge a little." As a salad, Mami has cut tomatoes and

From left: Guada, Mami, Teti, Vero, and I
at home on top of Casa Lau (circa 1975).

cucumbers on top of which she has squeezed some limes and sprinkled a bit of salt. Mami asks me to serve us each a bowl of freshly cooked rice, as she cannot resist eating rice. *"Ngo yateng yiu sek fan"* ("I must always eat rice, at every meal"), she says.

Mami has also made some *caldo de pescado* (fish soup) because, ever since I can remember, we have always had to have soup for breakfast, lunch, and dinner. Mami would always say in her Chinese accent, *"Teti semple tene que tene sopa"* ("Teti must have soup at every meal") and then, after Teti had died, she would say, *"Tu papá semple tene que tene sopa"* ("Your father must have soup at every meal").

When I was growing up, Mami would yell *a come* in Spanish, then *sek fan* in Chinese, indicating that lunch or dinner was ready. Then, one of us children would head to Teti's room, grab his hand, and take him to the table. Following that, we would go to my parents' room and tell Papito that food was ready. Mami would be scooping the main dishes onto big plates and placing them in the middle of the table. Mamita would be serving large bowls of soup for the adults and small ones for us kids. Guada most likely would be serving rice in bowls, and Vero would be walking to the table and placing a bowl with rice in front of each person.

The first bowl of rice would be placed in front of Teti; the next one would be for Papito, then Mami, then Mamita, and then the rest of us. Teti would start eating, followed by Papito and then the rest. Before eating, we girls would say the customary "eat rice" to each adult, always starting with Teti and following in the same order as the rice bowls had been served. Mami would always serve Teti and Papito the biggest or meatiest pieces of food. As the youngest ones, we would only be allowed to eat any pieces of food located in front of us (and only with completely clean chopsticks – no grains of rice or any small pieces of food could be stuck on them). But once in a while, Mami would spoil us and purposely place a chicken leg or a juicy piece of meat on the plate we were allowed to take from. Other times, it was Teti who would tell Mami to dig out some good pieces for us and place them in each of our bowls.

"In the old times when I was little," Mami says, "my father was very strict about table manners because this was a clear indication whether your parents had brought you up well or not. There were many rules you had to remember: no starting to eat before any adults; no talking at the table; no slouching; no leaning or elbows on the table; no spreading yourself all over the table but rather share the limited space with others; no taking food from areas of the dishes other than the ones in front of you, and no food stuck on your chopsticks when you pick up food from the main plates; no fidgeting; and no leaving anything in your bowls, even a single grain of rice."

"If any of us children did any of these things, my father would put his chopsticks together in his fist and hit the culprit's hand as hard as he could. You would have that mark on your hand for a long time to remember."

I laugh at the memory of Mamita teaching us all these table manners when we were little, repeating them day after day, meal after meal, especially because we were girls. Luckily, we never got Mami's father's severe treatment, since a single look from Papito would do it for us. And just listening to Mami made us make an extra effort to sit up straighter in our chairs. Though once in a while, Mami would mumble something about the war if we dared to leave a grain of rice in our bowls.

"You don't know how lucky you are right now. When we were running away from the Japanese, there was no food to eat. The only things we could find were shrubs, leaves, and bulbs in the fields. Whatever you could find, you would boil for a long time and that would be your meal."

All this must have made an impression since even now as an adult I do not have the heart to throw away any leftover food, which usually serves as my tasty lunch the following day. I also hate myself for leaving anything on my plate, whether it is a tiny grain of rice or a meagre crumb of bread.

After eating and before getting up to clear the table, I automatically address Mami with a polite *mah-man sek* ("eat slowly"). She surprisingly looks at me and responds with the same words. When we were kids, we had to say this expression to each adult at the table starting with Teti before being allowed to leave the table. I can only guess that Mami has not heard that expression in many years. She also has a look of exhaustion – probably from all the physical activity during the last few days combined with the heat and the 100% level of humidity.

I convince her to go to the living room and watch one of her soaps. She replies that her *telenovelas* are not on until later in the afternoon, but she is going to sit in front of the TV anyways and watch one of those star gossip programs with hostess Paty Chapoy. Now she has *Canal Dos, Canal Azteca*, and a few more channels to choose from. When I was growing up we only had three channels: *Canal Dos* (no competition with any other Mexican channel) which showed mostly soaps, variety shows, and news; *Canal 10 Cultural de México* (quite dull "cultural" programming); and *Canal 3* from Guatemala (since Tapachula was near the border), which showed dubbed American programs, such as *Perdidos en el Espacio* (Lost in Space), *Starsky y Hutch, Los Angeles de Charlie, El Doctor Quincy, La Isla de la Fantasía, CHIPs*, and cartoons like *Bugs Bunny, El Pato Donald, La Pantera Rosa, Speedy González*, and *El Correcaminos* (the Roadrunner).

Mami goes to the living room, turns the TV on, and sits in front of it falling in and out of sleep for the next hour or so. I escape to clean up the dishes and reminisce about when I was little and everyone took a siesta after lunch. I had the house all to myself to call friends, do homework, read, or do whatever I wanted as long as I was quiet.

Because Casa Lau is on top of a hill, no houses block our large windows and sliding doors. The house has always been breezy throughout the day. In addition to the breeze, I am also enjoying the stillness and relative quietness that siesta time brings to the city between 2:00 p.m. and 4:00 p.m.

At 4:00 p.m., before *Kam Long* closes for the day, Mami visits Tía Nelly and Ka-Yeh at their restaurant as she used to do daily before moving to Campeche. I decide to accompany her because I have not seen them in a while, and it is also a way of making sure Mami will arrive safely since she cannot see well and has difficulty walking, especially on the uneven sidewalks, built individually with different heights, slopes, and surfaces by each homeowner.

Tía Nelly and Ka-Yeh greet Mami ceremoniously, and I affectionately hug and kiss Tía Nelly and shake Ka-Yeh's hand. They ask me about my parents, and I ask them about their children whom I grew up with and call cousins. Next, we all sit down and they ask Mami and me if we are hungry and offer us something to drink. We refuse but they ask one of their waitresses to bring hot tea and two slices of *queso napolitano*, something similar to vanilla custard. Finally, the three of them talk in a lively way in *Kau Kong Wah* about issues in the city, what is going on in their lives and with their own families and about the latest news within the Chinese community; they chat, gossip, complain, laugh.

Mami pays Tía Nelly for buying her food at the market and asks her for a few additional items on her next trip. As always, they fight over money; Mami wants to pay a little extra, and Tía Nelly charges her less than what it costs or sometimes nothing at all. And if no one wins this argument, they trick each other by putting money into each other's pockets or hiding money in the items they have bought for each other.

After chatting for an hour or so, Mami and I leave with the bag full of food that Tía Nelly has bought and a couple of dishes she has made for us. Ever since I can remember, Tía Nelly has crossed the street between her home and ours to share cakes, pies, Chinese and Mexican dishes, fruits, vegetables, and any other foods she may have made or bought for her own family. And throughout the years, Mami has reciprocated in the same manner.

Kam Long is barely half a block away from Casa Lau on *la treceava poniente*. Though we are carrying all the food Tía Nelly has given us, Mami decides to head a couple of blocks eastbound away from Casa Lau, to where she used to buy sweet breads. We enter a narrow path into a small courtyard where an older lady sits after 5:00 or 6:00ish and sells freshly-baked Mexican sweet breads. There are all sorts of sweet breads in a round, big weaving basket, and the smell is too much for me to resist. So I grab a metal tray and tongs and choose *conchas, polvorones, sopes, azucaradas,* and Mami's favourite *michoacanas*, too many for only the two of us. After the woman places all the breads in a paper bag, we pay a couple of pesos and slowly walk back home.

On the way, I grab a *sope* made of molasses and eat it. Though I already know this, Mami reminds me once again that she no longer eats dinner and has a cup of coffee and either sweet bread or cookies instead.

"When we lived in Casa Lau, I used to make large suppers with rice and soup every night because of Teti and your father. But after I moved in with Tía Lupe, I stopped cooking and eating large meals at night. Not good for you to eat so much before going to bed. So are you going to be okay if I don't make anything in the evenings at all?"

"Mami, I'm going to be just fine. So why don't we have sweet breads for dinner tonight?" I respond. Mami sits with a cup of freshly-brewed Tapachula coffee and I with a mug of hot milk and a splash of coffee for colouring.

"Mami, do you know what happened with *la panadería Orozco*?" I ask her about the bread shop where we used to buy sweet breads.

"I heard people saying that one of the two sisters who owned and baked all the breads died, but I'm not sure. Their breads were the best in town: good and fresh. Too bad because they were in business for a long time and now you don't know where to go for bread. Everyone in Tapachula used to buy their breads in *la Orozco*. It didn't matter that the *panadería* was on a quiet street somewhere in the south of the city near *la Plaza de Toros* (an open air structure where bullfights and concerts were held) and away from everything. The Orozco sisters' breads were famous," Mami explains.

The smell of bread enveloped your senses the moment you drove onto their street. You entered through a long corridor with a large patio entrance full of colourful flowers. At the end of the house were huge ovens and large round wicker *canastas* scattered all over where freshly-baked, hot sweet breads piled up. After picking up a round metal tray and metal tongs, you would walk around the entire place first and then make a second round to pick the breads you wanted and needed to buy since the selection was large and the smell was intoxicating. If you went around 6:00 p.m. when the breads were coming out of the ovens, you could pick out yours from the endless trays that the *panaderos* placed on rows of carts to cool down before putting them in the wicker *canastas*. Very often you ended up eating a couple of small breads before reaching the cashier; you would then mention how many you and your companions had had and the cashier would add them to your final tab. It was a delicious outing.

8

FROM KAU KONG
TO SAN SALVADOR

IT is 6:00 a.m. and I wake up with the sun shining brightly
and clear, blue skies. It is hard to stay in bed when I know
Mami is already somewhere in the house cooking and
cleaning. Anyhow, I am looking forward to some *tamales* for
breakfast. When we arrived, I had mentioned to Tía Elda
that I was hoping I could eat some *tamales*. So, she put in an
order with a woman who makes them in her neighbourhood,
and last night, Tía Elda came by to drop off a variety of
tamales de chipilín (made with a green vegetable indigenous
to the area), *tamales de cambray* (sweet tamales), and my
all-time favourite *tamales de elote* (made of fresh corn, milk,
and butter) which are difficult to find this time of the year
because it is not the season to harvest sweet corn.

But suddenly I remember that I need to find out if
Mamita's washing machine is working. This is probably the
second washing machine we have had, and both easily broke
down because of irregular electrical power surges. I recall
turning on and off the regulator for our big television console
when I was growing up so that the TV would not be damaged.

Mami washes her clothes by hand like she has always done. She has never liked anybody doing it for her and never used a washing machine. When we were little, we had a live-in maid who babysat us, cleaned the house, and washed our clothes. As we got older, we no longer needed maids and house chores were simply divided. We three girls took turns every Saturday dusting, sweeping, and mopping the living room, dining rooms, and kitchen and cleaning the three bathrooms. We were also in charge of our own bedrooms, Mami and Teti's, and Tío Juanca's (where Teti used to take his afternoon naps). But the room my parents shared was always off-limits.

By the time I was in eighth grade, Papito had bought Mamita a washing machine for large items such as sheets, towels, and tablecloths. Eventually, Mamita used her machine to wash everyone's clothes except Mami's. Guada and I took turns hanging them on the clotheslines, taking the dry ones down, folding them, and ironing Papito and Teti's undershirts, underwear, and handkerchiefs. Mami never dared to even touch the washing machine for fear of pushing the wrong button or breaking it.

This time is no different; I catch her washing her clothes with some mixture of old broken bags of colourful dish powder and clothing detergents, which we could not sell in the store. So I tell her that I have wiped all the dust and spider webs off the clothesline, and that I will go up to the roof to hang her clothes for her. The staircase is quite steep, and I am afraid she might fall down. She nods in agreement and continues washing her clothes, while I go and inspect Mamita's washing machine. As I recall, the machine will work just fine as long as the large main water tank is full of water, and I use it during the daytime when usually there are no power outages or surges because of low demand.

After ensuring the machine is running properly, I head to the table where Mami has already warmed up three *tamales*, one of each kind for me to share with her. There is also a paper bag full of churros, which I plan to snack on all day. I open up the banana leaves and serve the *tamal de chipilín* and the *tamal de cambray*. After she finishes, Mami tells me to eat the *tamal de elote* by myself since she knows how much I like them and because I cannot get them in Canada. So I slowly open up the corn shells, let the *tamal* out on the plate, pour some cream and crumble some cheese, and savour it.

Between bites, Mami tells me she will teach me how to make *tou sah pau*, sweet bean paste steamed buns. I only like it the way she makes the paste with black beans (not red beans as in the real Chinese way). Plus, red beans are hard to come by in Tapachula. Making buns and paste is so time-consuming that I automatically start thinking that I am never going to have the time or space in Vancouver to make either from scratch. But as Mami has always said, "You have to learn how to cook everything in case you end up living in a place where you cannot easily buy these foods already prepared."

The washing machine works perfectly, and after it stops, I take my clothes and some large towels to the clothesline on the roof. That is when I discover that Mami has already climbed the unsafe, green metal staircase and hung her clothes neatly on the clothesline to dry. I cannot really get mad at her for trying to do what she has always done. I shake my head, realizing that she is as stubborn as always and that I simply have to keep a closer eye on her and try to outsmart her, just like she is trying to do with me.

Besides washing her clothes, Mami has spent all morning in her *oficina* setting everything up to make *tou sah pau*. She spent three hours yesterday, after we came back from the bread shop, boiling the black beans, grinding them, and finally cooking them slowly with sugar and oil until they have turned into a delicious and smooth paste. She did all this because the *tou sah* or bean paste needs to be chilled before using it as stuffing for the buns.

After mixing flour, oil, and yeast with water at the right temperature and adding a bit of sugar, she kneads the mixture, covers it, and waits. Then, she kneads it once again, covers it, and waits for the dough to rise to the consistency and fluffiness she likes. She tests the dough by tapping and squeezing it.

"Do the same as I do. You have to learn and remember

how the right consistency should feel. This way, you don't need exact measurements."

When it is perfect, she cuts the dough into small squares, rounds, and spreads them all over the table. I now join her in flattening the little pieces of dough, stuffing them with sweet black bean paste, shaping them into balls, and pushing the ends together into one seam to create a nice round bun. Then we slap a square of white *papel china* or rice paper (about two inches by two inches) onto the seam so the paste stays inside and the bun does not stick onto the pan when it is steamed. We place the finished bun in the mesh bottom of round aluminum pans, made to Mami's specifications, and keep shaping and stuffing buns while she tells me what happened after the war.

"After living briefly in the third floor apartment in Kong Chau, Tai-Ku, Papito, and I moved to a small house with two bedrooms. This was further away but cheaper. I continued working at Ah-Bun's shop, and Papito stayed with Tai-Ku when not in school. This was a peaceful and worry-free time for me. The war was over; we had a place to live and did not have to move constantly. I had reconnected with Teti, who was sending us money, and we had something more substantial to eat than bulbs and weeds. But for Papito these were probably still hard times because he was a precocious eight-year-old without a father. We were still living under extremely poor conditions, and I know he was constantly hungry and deprived of many of the basic things that most children would have had before the war: toys, books, and kids to play with."

"About a year later, some of the Chinese men who had gone to Tapachula were returning with their children. In Kong Chau, I met Gustavo Lau, one of Teti's nephews who had almost gambled Casa Lau away. He was traveling with his two children, Pek-Fong and Chan-Kei, who ended up staying in Hong Kong where they eventually made their own lives. Another Chinese man from the Lau clan whom Teti had originally sponsored was Tía Nelly's father. Though he worked at another Chinese-owned store, he returned to Casa Lau every day to eat his meals. He had married Tía Chusita (a compassionate Mexican lady of very strong character) and was bringing his three Mexican-born children, Tía Nelly, Tía Blanqui, and Ah-Ming-Suk back to learn the language. They were very young when they arrived and lived briefly in Kong Chau. Ah-Bun and I went to the airport in Hong Kong to greet them. It was the first time I met them."

Mami, her sister-in-law Tai-Ku, and Papito eventually moved back to Kau Kong. And with money Mami had saved and money Teti had sent from Tapachula, she was able to purchase their first newly-built home, which has been kept and maintained in Kau Kong and which Mami still holds onto dearly.

I recall from my visit a few years back that it is a small, two-storey house with a courtyard, allowing access to the kitchen and the bathroom. Next to the kitchen there is another door into the living room and dining room areas. A narrow, wooden staircase leads up to the second floor, where there are two bedrooms.

Mami's house in Kau Kong (late 1960s).

Dust had collected on the pieces of Chinese-style solid cherry furniture still standing still in the master bedroom and in the living room and dining room. There were only a few pots and pans in the kitchen, and there were sets of paintings hanging on the walls of the living room; one of an older bearded man, another of an elderly woman, and a third one of an elderly couple, all gazing seriously outward. There was a familial resemblance; they were most likely either Mami's or Teti's parents or grandparents.

As I get up for some drinking water, I take advantage of the break and run to look for the pictures I managed to take of Mami's house. She looks intently with much interest at some of these photos, which I remember having difficulty taking since the house was small and dark. Mami asks me many questions, and I try my best to answer so she gets a clear idea of where everything is. She is relieved that nothing seems changed, that the house seems exactly the same with each piece of furniture in the same spot. However, when we start talking about the surroundings, a different picture emerges.

"When I bought my house in Kau Kong, it was a quiet neighbourhood and considered to be the outskirts of town. Behind the house, there was a pond full of large golden fish and nothing else."

"Mami, the pond has now been replaced," I say, "by rows of houses that stand one next to another. The town has grown and things are definitely very different."

Mami hands me back the pictures and says, "My house was considered quite modern for the times when I purchased it because it had an indoor bathroom. Can you imagine a bathroom - and indoors? It was extremely difficult to buy because I didn't have a lot of money and I didn't know anything. It was my first house. So to me, buying it was a great accomplishment. Did you meet my mother's *yeung noi*? She is the one who has keys and keeps the house clean and fairly well-maintained. She wrote to me a long time ago and has told Papito that the house has been flooded a few times during the heavy rains in the fall."

Mami looks at my puzzled face and asks, "Do you know what a *yeung noi* is?"

"Not really," I respond. "But now that you mention it, I remember seeing the horizontal lines and marks left outside your house because of the floods."

"My mother used to have a few young girls at home who helped out with the house chores. These girls were sold off from very poor families who could not afford to feed another person. Some girls were sold into families who mistreated them and never allowed them to leave unless some payment was made. At our home, though, my mother taught them everything about how to run a household, and in exchange for their work they received food and a place to stay. My father even provided schooling to the girls who sometimes wanted more than just learning to cook and clean."

"Throughout the years, I recall my mother having three *yeung noi*. They all remained with her for a long time before being married off one by one. All of them developed a mutual caring relationship with some of us siblings, but undoubtedly there was a special bond and loyalty towards my mother. The last girl my mother had as *yeung noi* is the woman who now takes care of my house in Kau Kong. She cleans the house and makes sure everything is okay and lets your Papito know if something is not. We have known each other for a long time and she is a trustworthy and hard-working lady. She is probably ten or more years younger than I am."

"I remember her. With so many relatives I haven't met, I had assumed she was one of Papito's cousins. We met her in her apartment, and she offered us tea. Then we walked over to your house. She opened up all the rooms for us to inspect. I thought she was in her 60's but it is very hard to say because she had a very young-looking face," I finally respond.

While I put everything away (including the leftover bean paste which I place in the fridge and scoop out as a snack in the days that follow), Mami prepares to cook the buns, which have been evenly distributed on eight aluminum mesh-bottom trays. Mami had the trays especially made to steam Chinese buns stuffed with chicken, pork, or sweet bean paste. I carefully light the stone stove and place an oversize *wok* with water on top of it. Then I place the trays on a tree-like metal-rod structure, and the entire assembly goes into the *wok*. Then I cover this with a large upside-down pot. Since it holds four large round trays, we will cook all the buns in two batches. Mami tells me she will let me know when the buns are done so we can take the trays out and let the *tou sah pau* cool down.

In the meantime, Mami makes deep-fried, Kau Kong-style spring rolls for lunch. She has cut vegetables and chicken into fine thin strips, marinated and then rolled them in very delicate, pig stomach lining sheets. She keeps two rolls for us and the rest, along with a few sweet bean buns, we will deliver to Tía Nelly, Tío Neto, and Mami's doctor Fernando. Next, she asks me to call Tío Carlos and Tía Elda to come by and pick some up because she knows they really like them. Then Mami also puts three steamed buns and a couple of spring rolls on a plate in front of Teti and Tío Pepe's black-and-white pictures and lights a candle.

Mami also deep-fries prawns in the oil so it does not go to waste after one use, using a flour batter she makes from scratch. She tells me that the secret for getting a fluffy and crunchy consistency is to chill the batter in ice. Then with guilty eyes, she says that she does not usually have rolls or this type of fried prawns since they are unhealthy, *"Hou fei poco hou sek"* ("they are fatty, but yummy"). Then she switches to Spanish, saying that she has *antojo* (craving) since she has not had either of these oily dishes in a long time. With rice, Kau

Kong-style spring rolls and deep-fried prawns, we sit down to eat at 2:00 p.m. and Mami continues her story.

"Tía Nelly's father was also from Kau Kong. Shortly after Tai-Ku, Papito, and I returned to Kau Kong, Tía Nelly, Tía Blanqui, and Ah-Ming-Suk left Kong Chau to live in Kau Kong with their aunt [their father's sister]. She took care of them and they developed an almost mother-like relationship with her. The three siblings stayed and studied in China for approximately eleven years."

"Tai-Ku lived briefly in Kau Kong and then joined her grown son in Hong Kong. She decided to help find a suitable wife for him. After her son married, she lived in Hong Kong with him for the remainder of her long and peaceful life. Papito and I stayed in Kau Kong, where Papito continued studying very hard. He loved reading and studying and was extremely good at school. He just wanted to learn everything and anything. And he never asked me for help with his homework. I think Papito inherited his love for books from Teti."

"After we were living on our own in Kau Kong, I received a message from Teti that he was coming back to China. According to him, China was not totally safe and was still in political turmoil. Because of the feeling of uncertainty still lingering after the war, Teti bought an apartment on the Kowloon side. So Papito and I rushed to Hong Kong to meet up with him. We were so afraid of being split up again. After ten long years, this was the first time I had a husband by my side and Papito a father. I was very happy."

"Because of what had happened with Casa Lau during his first trip back to find a wife, Teti was afraid to leave the store with his nephews for too long. After almost a year in Kowloon, Teti headed back to Tapachula. This time, he took us back with him. It was Papito and I, and my nephew, the son of my brother #10; he wanted to work outside of China. We needed to pay for flights for three adults and one child. When we were ready to leave, Teti couldn't access the funds that his nephews had transferred from Tapachula. We were desperate, and Teti looked for loans without any success. Finally, I had to sell the few things I had left and took out most of my savings to be able to gather enough money to buy all four tickets. It's good to be frugal; you never know when you're going to need every penny you have. It was because I have the habit to save and not spend that got us out of trouble again."

"Teti left for Mexico while the three of us (Papito, my nephew, and I) headed to San Salvador (in El Salvador) where our travelling papers were waiting. Papito's were all in order because he was Teti's son. So were my nephew's because he was sponsored as a worker for Casa Lau under the name of Ramón. But mine were taking a bit longer to process since it was complicated. Teti had made arrangements to buy a birth certificate for me from a Chinese Salvadorean whose daughter was deceased. That meant that I would have to adopt a new identity, entering Mexico as a Salvadorean. I didn't know I had to do this until we were in El Salvador. I had no other choice."

This was a risky decision, but it was the only way to get Mami "legally" into Mexico because, at the time, the Mexican government would only allow Chinese males into the country through an employer or a family sponsorship program. And the number of Chinese females allowed was extremely small and under specific circumstances that were costly, time-consuming, and cumbersome.

"I was very worried because my new papers showed the age of a girl much younger than I was. The Chinese Salvadorean *paisano* who had sold Teti my birth certificate kept telling me that all Chinese looked alike to most Mexicans so there was nothing to be worried about. As long as I correctly answered all of the Immigration authorities' questions, getting through would not be a problem. So this raised a bigger problem because I spoke no Spanish. What if the Immigration agent asked me a different question from my name, age, and date of birth? I was very worried."

"We stayed in San Salvador for about fifteen days at the *paisano's* house, and there was another Chinese woman living there who was waiting for her papers, too (she was going to Tapachula as well). Poor woman! She had been waiting for a longer time because her husband was having difficulty gathering enough money to pay for her release. I felt so bad for her that once Teti paid for our transport to Mexico, I gave the woman the loan she needed. She was freed soon after."

"Days later and with papers in hand, the *paisano* drove me, Papito, and Ramón, to Guatemala, where we took a plane to Mexico City and entered the country without any problems. I felt so relieved and thought that I had worried for nothing. Then we took another plane to our final destination to meet Teti. Finally, I could breathe a little easier."

9

COMMUNITY LIFE
IN TAPACHULA

GROWING up Chinese in Tapachula was something I took as normal; I never thought there was anything peculiar or unusual about it. But since then I have come to realize that our tightknit community of *paisanos* was different, and that we represented the exception rather than the norm. As a community, we held special celebrations and had our own social gatherings ranging from weekends at Don Manuel's beach lot to birthday parties, communions, weddings, and visits to each other's homes. From this group of family and friends, we acquired and shared common beliefs, cultural traditions, and specific ways of doing things.

Everyone helped one another out, either by taking and picking up each other's children from school, or by sharing dishes when somebody made something special with difficult-to-find ingredients. The camaraderie went beyond and was deeper; we supported one another instead of competing against even when families were in exactly the same line of business, whether it was a grocery store, a restaurant, a clothing store, or a ranch struggling to produce cotton or soybeans.

The community shared many traits that contrasted with the "normal" social fabric of Mexico. We were not only physically similar to each other (and therefore different from the rest of the population in Tapachula), but most of the older generation spoke Chinese and maintained a tight link with a faraway family in China. Perhaps this closeness arose out of a common need since many years ago our grandparents and parents had arrived without being able to speak Spanish or knowing anything about their new Mexican homeland. They shared the common goal of finding success by working hard and enjoying the product of their work. Their reliance on each other was elementary and instinctive since their similarities superseded their differences, and their united front helped them cope with the difficulties of being alone in an unfamiliar place. As the offspring of first- or second-generation immigrants, we were born into this closeness and group reliance.

All these characteristics set us apart and somehow at some time the word *paisano*, which means "countryman" in Spanish, began to be used in reference to a person of Chinese descent or associated with the Chinese community, in particularly in Tapachula and nearby areas. *Paisano* is still a preferred term in our community, denoting positive images of the classical hard-working, serious, studious, honest Chinese. By contrast, the harsh-sounding word *chino*, or Chinese, carries negative connotations and is used by

Mami and Teti attending a church wedding ceremony
of a member of the Chinese community
as padrinos de velación, or main witnesses
(mid 1970s).

outsiders when trying to be demeaning and offensive in Tapachula and its surroundings, but nowhere else in Mexico. As a child, I knew the difference when somebody called me *paisana* or *china*. Even now as an adult, I unconsciously cringe when I hear *china*; instead, I prefer *paisana* or the softer diminutive Chinese *chinita*.

At the same time, *paisanos* were never segregated or ghettoized. We lived wherever we wanted and were not confined to a specific part of Tapachula. In fact, we have combined cultures, shared traditions, and been part of the social fabric of the city to the point that Chinese food is considered customary and *paisanos* continue to play as significant and essential a role as anybody else in Tapachula.

Although Mami never talked about it (because that simply was not done), she was very proud of Teti's role in the community. He believed that it was his responsibility to give back and make sure that, as a *paisano*, he played an important role and kept a good and positive image. He supported all the Chinese community's causes and strongly emphasized the importance of opening and maintaining a school to teach the Chinese language. He also joined other Chinese businessmen to build a public park with a Chinese theme so that all of Tapachula's residents could enjoy and get to know a bit about our Chinese culture. Our community also worked tirelessly to build and fully furnish a much-needed public elementary school, now called *Lázaro Cárdenas*, which still operates.

And they even contributed to buy wood furniture from China for the city mayor's office as a token of appreciation for welcoming Chinese immigration.

Teti (first on the left) with city officials attending a groundbreaking ceremony in Tapachula (unknown date).

Teti also lent money and merchandise (without ever asking for any of it back) to struggling families who were trying to make ends meet. He also extended credit to some corner stores as well as mom-and-pop stores and allowed them to pay him back on their own time. Teti was chosen to be a *consejero* for the Board of Directors of *Bancomer* or *Banco de Comercio* and served for many decades. This was a very prestigious position which was only offered to major contributors to the Tapachula business community. As Mami says, Teti was the best man she could have ever imagined marrying.

When I was younger and Mami made something special, usually a Chinese delicacy that was labour-intensive, she would make enough to distribute not only to Tía Nelly, Tía Elda, and Tío Neto and his wife Vicky, but also to some of our neighbouring *paisanos* like the Joos and the Puongs. Now I understand why.

Mami playing mah-jong at the beach
near Tapachula (mid 1950s).

Mami played *mah-jong* with some of the *paisanas* who lived closer to the centre of town. Doña Lupe, who was married to a *paisano* and interested in all aspects of Chinese culture, befriended Mami and became a *keok* or a "foot" whenever the older ladies did not have the customary four players. Mami appreciated Doña Lupe's sense of humour and warm laughter and included her whenever the rounds of food delivery were made.

Doña Mari de Joo was also a Mexican woman who was considered a *paisana* after marrying Don Félix Joo. They lived with their thirteen children across the street from the Puongs. Like Tía Nelly's family the Macks, Tía Blanqui's family the Cincos, the Puongs, and us the Laus, the Joos owned and managed a small *tienda de abarrotes* on this side of *la octava*. In addition, they had a *cantina* next to their grocery store. Being neighbours and having children around the same age, Doña Mari and Mami (whose name was also María) had a special affection and respect for each other. Throughout the years, Mami would send Doña Mari her Chinese specialties. And Doña Mari would do the same by sending us some of her famous *carne asada* grilled with a splash of beer on hot charcoals and handmade tortillas. During harvest, Doña Mari would also have one of her kids bring different types of mangoes from the family ranch as well as sacks of freshly-cut tamarind so we could make *aguas* or drinks mixed with water and sugar.

This afternoon, everyone is very thankful to Mami for receiving the buns and the spring rolls. But unfortunately there is only one portion left for Doña Mari's son, Doctor Fernando Joo. He works throughout the day at the *Seguro Social*, the government-run hospital, but during siesta time and mostly in the late evenings he sees patients in his office (located on the other side of the street in front of Tía Nelly's house), where his family used to have their grocery store and *cantina*. Mami tells me he is a doctor like no other, very caring, a good listener, and still making house calls when patients feel so sick they cannot come to the hospital or office. He also refuses to charge family members, close friends, and patients with no financial means. So Doctor Fernando gets a lot of food and gifts, as well as admiration and respect from many people around the community. Mami cannot believe she has known Fernando all his life and is pleased to have seen him grow into a fine person and doctor.

It is 8:30 p.m. when I look out from our front patio and see that the metal curtains in his office are drawn, a sign that he is open for business. So we head out and cross the street. The young receptionist seated on a chair in front of a small desk looks up, tells us that the doctor is not in yet, and asks us to take a seat. The room is small, with a few wooden chairs for patients and a partition that separates the waiting area from the examination area. Luckily, we are the first patients in the room.

A few minutes later, Doctor Fernando walks in, very effusively says hello, and beckons us to follow him in. He takes a seat behind his desk and gestures to us to sit across from him on two wooden chairs. As we talk and catch up, he listens to Mami's heart and measures her blood pressure. Then, he returns to his desk and using his two index fingers types a note for Mami to buy sleeping pills. After signing it, he hands it to Mami and also gives her a couple of bottles of cough medicine from his medication cabinet. He tells me that Mami is doing very well health-wise and reminds her to have half a sleeping pill every night and double the dose if needed since it is very important that she get some rest, which she has not had much of lately.

After chatting for a while, Mami hands Doctor Fernando the plate of spring rolls and Chinese buns. He is thrilled since he has not had any of these since Mami made them a few years back. As we leave, we notice that the waiting room is packed with patients, some of them even standing outside on the sidewalk and a few more sitting on the hood of a parked car. The doctor signals the receptionist not to charge us anything, while Mami slips her a bill and tells her that it is payment for the visit.

The next morning Mami and I have crispy *pan francés* for breakfast, our version of French bread but shaped like two five-inch long mini baguettes glued together side by side. We dip them into a steaming bowl of *atole de elote* (sweet corn porridge), eating the soft doughy core first and leaving the crispy shell for last. At this moment, we look like two young kids opening presents on Christmas Day. Tía Nelly has asked one of her restaurant helpers bring over the porridge as well as some fresh *robalo* fish that Mami had ordered from the market for lunch.

I smile at Mami and remind her that we are only two in Casa Lau so she does not, once again, make food for an army since I feel my pants are a bit tighter than when we first arrived. But after breakfast, Mami tells me she is planning lunch already.

As usual, she gets ready to make food forgetting about everything else around her. She clears the table and gets her tools to filet the fish. She gets rid of the skin and the bones, and then she holds two Chinese cleavers, one in each hand, and chops endlessly until the filets become a fish paste. She adds a little salty water here and there, and when she likes the starchy consistency, she puts in pre-soaked thinly-sliced dried Chinese mushrooms, evenly cut *cilantro*, and other herbs and condiments. She then throws and kneads and throws the paste back and forth against a stainless steel bowl. Meanwhile, I cut, clean, and get rid of the seeds of a few green peppers and some hot *jalapeños*. I also peel, cut, and wash a couple of eggplants.

When everything is done, Mami stuffs all the vegetables with the fish paste and places them on a plate. Then she puts carefully each stuffed piece on a hot *wok* and browns both the fish side and the vegetable side. Then she seasons this dish with soy sauce, rice wine, sugar, and ginger and thickens it with cornstarch and water. She also stirfries some *chicoria*, or Chinese cabbage, with dried scallops which she says Papito had brought for her on his last trip from Vancouver. She reminds me that her favourite vegetable is *chicoria*, which unfortunately she cannot get in Campeche, so she will try to eat as much as she can while we are here.

While sitting in the kitchen with Mami, I feel that time has passed without much of anything really changing around Casa Lau. There is still the constant breeze I always felt in this house because of its location. The floor still shakes every time a truck or a bus passes by. The delicious fragrances from Mami's constant culinary creations, combined with the delicious smell of tacos emanating from the street vendors below are also still present. Familiar utensils, dishes, pots, and pans stand, all lined up and on top of each other, in the same cabinets and drawers where they have always been.

There is also an uncanny familiarity in the sounds I hear. There is the constant stream of cars going by with their different-sounding horns: taxi drivers honking at pedestrians signaling they are *libres* (available), drivers happily sounding their horns when they see someone familiar walk by, and a third kind of driver honking annoyingly, non-stop, and yelling obscenities at an old pedestrian running for his life to cross *la octava* below.

I can also hear the voices of women chanting about whatever they are selling, as they walk the uneven sidewalks below. Their heads balance heavy, woven baskets full of fruits and vegetables (with only a rolled up piece of cloth serving as cushion), and they usually carry a small child tightly wrapped and tied around their bodies with a colourful *reboso*.

I can hear the young boys going up and down the street yelling "*el Diario, el Diario del Sur*," the daily local newspaper. I can hear the loud music of *mariachis* mixed with *marimbas* and jukeboxes playing *norteñas* and *tropicales* from a couple of bars nearby. And I can still hear the roosters that, contrary to popular belief, crow at any time of the day, all day long.

10

EVERYDAY LIFE
IN TAPACHULA

FOR a change, this morning Mami and I slowly walk to the market. I hold onto her arm tightly since going down the steep street beside our house is no easy task even for me. But Mami is determined because she wants to buy some items that, according to her, only she knows where to find. It is busy, noisy, and smelly but Mami is all eyes for various Chinese vegetables and for the yellow-skin free-range chickens and the clear-eyed fresh fish.

"I didn't like it here when I first came to this country," Mami says. "I remember driving from the small airport thinking this was not a very civilized place. The road was dusty and not paved, and the jungle was all over. There were animals on the road also."

"Oh, it couldn't have been that bad," I joke with her.

"Yes, it was," she responds quickly. "I kept looking for buildings and people but not much was going on. And when we crossed the city, I realized Tapachula was tinier than a small town in China and had very few paved streets. The worst was that Casa Lau was at the end of one of these paved streets. There was nothing behind or beside us, only jungle. At night, I was so afraid because darkness and silence surrounded us. There was nothing to do or see in Tapachula."

"What year was this, Mami?"

"Late 1949. It was a long and difficult trip, and worst of all, I was seven months pregnant, so I felt sick and tired all the time. And since Casa Lau was not ready for our arrival, we stayed for a few days with Don José Chong. He was a well-known Chinese businessman who owned one of the largest trading companies closer to the centre of town. Everybody respected him because he sponsored and welcomed many new Chinese to Tapachula."

"Meanwhile, Teti hired somebody to build a small room and added a few extra beds to the warehouse next to where sacks of salt used to be stored. But this was just two pieces of wood for walls put up against a corner that didn't even reach the ceiling. And my bedroom was very noisy, and at night I was afraid of the rain hitting the roof and the sound of the trees and the bushes brushing against the back walls of the store or the howling and fighting of stray dogs. I always had a hard time falling asleep, but it was a luxury compared to where we had slept during the war."

As Mami and I walk past the market stalls, I decide to indulge in a few things (hoping I will not get sick). I buy a cold drink called *choco milk* made with milk, chocolate powder, cinnamon, and lots of sugar and ice which I used to get when I was younger. These are still served in a plastic bag with a straw, just like any other cold drink to go, like a shake, fruit juice, or cold, bottled sodas. As we walk by, we see a few carts on wheels where they serve tasty hot dogs with *pambazo* bread, sausages cooked in water, mayo, ketchup, fresh tomatoes, onions, and spicy *jalapeño* peppers.

"A few months after we arrived in Tapachula," Mami continues, "our second son was born and we named him Pedrito. He was so healthy at first, but days later, he fell seriously ill, and I didn't know what to do. I was in a lot of distress and feeling very weak myself, and Pedrito didn't recover. I think about it and still do not understand what he died of, and the guilt of not being strong and not knowing enough to properly care for him has followed me like a shadow even until now."

We both have tears in our eyes, so I hold Mami's arm even tighter trying to comfort her.

"Then two and a half years later," Mami continues, "my nephew Ramón passed away from cancer. He had many protrusions all over his neck. At first they did not hurt; but afterwards when the pain was too much, he went to Mexico City. Teti arranged with a *paisano* who was on his way to Mexico to see a doctor to take my nephew along. So they took the plane together and checked into a hotel. But the following day when they were to meet for breakfast, Ramón didn't show up. The *paisano* decided to knock on his door and discovered that my nephew was already dead. He was so young, barely twenty-three years old. He is the boy buried in the *panteón* almost behind Teti's grave."

But there was no time or chance to feel sad or depressed. Mami was pregnant three more times, each time soon after the previous time. In 1951 she had Tía Chony and Tío Pepe, twins. Tía Lupe's birth followed in early 1953. Then a year and a half after the death of Ramón, Tío Juanca was born in 1954. This was the toughest delivery because Mami lost a lot of blood. So the doctor recommended surgery to prevent her getting pregnant again. But Teti refused to consider what, at that time, he called an extreme procedure. Mami tried the pill for a short period, but it gave her severe headaches. Then, for some unexplained reason, she suddenly stopped menstruating altogether. Mami felt relieved, and though he never said anything of the sort, Mami thinks Teti was relieved, too.

During these difficult times, Mami met and became best friends with a Mexican lady, Doña Angela who was kind and patient and accompanied Mami everywhere. Doña Angela spent endless nights comforting Mami through pregnancies and deliveries and during painful events. And in spite of the language barrier, they developed a deep friendship, which has lasted many years. Until a few years ago, Mami and Doña Angela visited each other whenever possible. Even now, though they live more than 1400 kilometres away in

Querétaro, both Tía Chony and Doña Angela's son Edy have maintained contact.

As Mami and I pass by other food stands, I cannot resist the temptation of buying some *jobos* and *nances*, tropical fruits from the region preserved in sweet alcohol. Even though it is too early for any stomach, I grab a bag of chunks of green mangoes soaked in lime juice and chili powder. There are pieces of watermelons, coconuts, honeydews, and oranges as well, but I know I cannot get green mangoes in Vancouver so I go for those. Mami looks at me with disapproval, so I assure her that I will keep everything, except for my *choco milk* for after lunch.

Mami tells me that when my uncles and aunts were small, she had one live-in nanny for each child in addition to a maid who cleaned the house and washed clothes. Like most large and established Chinese-run businesses, Casa Lau also had a Chinese cook.

"We had one young girl to look after each kid and a maid to clean and also had Mincho, who cooked Chinese food only and whom I used to watch and learn from because he never wanted to teach anybody. So I had to make casual conversation, watch him, and remember entire recipes. I think he was so secretive about his cooking because he was afraid to lose his job. But the truth is that all I wanted to do was to learn how to cook because I liked it."

Mincho had arrived in Tapachula at an early age, worked

in grocery stores and after many years owned one in a nearby *finca* with coffee plantations. Eventually, he got married and had a daughter. When she grew up and got married, Mincho decided to leave her the store and move back to Tapachula. Since he made excellent Chinese dishes and enjoyed doing this, he asked Teti for work in the kitchen as a cook. So Teti put Mincho in charge of cooking for everyone in Casa Lau and for some other *paisanos* who came to gather and have their daily meals. He cooked for many years after Mami's arrival and even after Mamita first arrived in Tapachula. He then retired from cooking in the late 1960s, and not long after, died from complications of kidney disease.

Besides keeping an eye on Mincho and trying to learn the secrets of his Chinese cooking, Mami was busy all the time making sure the household ran smoothly. She was vigilant about making sure that the children were well looked after and she took care of all four youngsters when the nannies were off at night and on Sundays. She also ensured that enough food was cooked for everyone and that the maid completed all cleaning chores efficiently and properly. When we talk about this time of her life, Mami tells me there is something she truly regrets. "From the time the kids were small, I always spoke to them in my broken Spanish. Why didn't I speak Chinese to them? I could have taught them and corrected them and perhaps we could have communicated better. Instead and for some reason I don't really understand,

I always spoke *ah kau kau* [in chunks] Spanish and even worse, I used bad Spanish. *Ah, yaah,* I didn't know anything better at the time."

"But your Dad was a quick learner and an avid student; so he progressed very quickly. And he loved reading books. Although he had not had much schooling and spoke no Spanish, he did a year or so of elementary school in Tapachula and then decided to go to Mexico City to do secondary and high school [in *Escuela Franco Español*]. A couple of years later, he finished studying something related to public accounting [at the *Instituto Washington*]. So for the first time in his short life, Papito and I were separated. But I was happy

Papito (first row in the middle) in Mexico City with friends and schoolmates (mid 1950s).

to see that he finally got to concentrate solely on schoolwork, like any young man his age should."

Mami's social life centred around the children. She rarely went out; when she did, it was to visit *paisanas* who had children about the same age as hers. She visited our neighbours Tía Chusita, the Joo Reyes family, and other friends who lived a few blocks away, like Doña Angela up the street. Once in a while Mami also stopped by to chat with Tía Chepina from the Pang Tangs and Doña Fanny from the Lamshings. Both families owned fabric stores in the centre of town. On her way home, she would quickly say hello and wave to the Corlays, the Loos, and the Changs, Chinese families with grocery stores on *la octava* but closer to the *parque central*.

Mami got to know all the *paisanas* and their families, and they became a close-knit community, holding each other's kids' *piñata* parties, celebrating Chinese New Year and their children's baptisms and communions together. Mami, Tía Chusita, Doña Angela, and Tía Chepina called each other *comadre*, which was customary when they became godmothers to each other's kids. Aside from respectfully addressing the older generation of adults as *Don* or *Doña*, most offspring within the community also used *Tío* and *Tía*, or *Padrino* and *Madrina* (godfather and godmother).

"Because of Teti, we received many invitations to community gatherings and dances for fundraising, most of

Mami and Tía Chepina
attending a wedding in the
Chinese community (unknown date).

which I did not attend. I didn't like going out and always felt that I didn't know how to make conversation. I also thought it really was a waste of time to go to the dances with their live bands and *marimbas* and *mariachis* because I didn't know how to dance, nor did I understand or appreciate the songs, and to top it off I hated loud music and still do."

"When I was growing up, you often said, '*Msik kong yeh yau msik kong mat'* [I don't know how to talk or what to say], whenever you didn't want to go out."

Mami laughs, shakes her head, and adds, "I learned to like some of the Mexican parties, especially the ones that had some religious meaning. I never missed the *sentadas de niño* or the *posadas* that Tía Chusi and Doña Angela used to organize in their homes. And I really like the gatherings with the cutting of *la rosca de reyes* [in January for the Magi] and even adopted some celebrations around *el día del muerto* in November, when I made special foods and took them to the cemetery. The children painted and stuffed egg shells with confetti or flour and cracked these on their friends' heads. I had never seen anything like this. The best part was the food people made for these festive occasions like *dulce de calabaza* [pumpkin cooked in molasses], *pan de muerto* [bread of the dead], and *hojuelas con miel* [deep-fried flat pastries served with red-coloured honey]."

As Mami and I quickly pass by the food stands, we see customers sitting on wooden stools drinking Coca Colas from glass bottles while waiting to be served. And we smell all kinds of *tacos, enchiladas,* and other fried fast foods, *fritangas,* being prepared and sold. We also notice with some surprise that a few stands are selling *chop suey, chow mein,* and *kai teng.* But instead of stopping to inspect any further, we head home before it gets too hot for Mami.

"I also enjoyed," Mami continues, "watching from our front patio the yearly city parade. We had the best seats because it passed by *la octava.* The parade was special because the *paisanos* participated with the Dragon and the Lion Dances. On occasion, a couple of men dressed up by covering themselves with a white sheet. They walked around with a fan in one hand and in the other a large, shiny, bald, red-cheeked Chinese papier maché head, teasing and taunting spectators. This event brought the entire Chinese community together. The elders taught the younger ones the dances, and everyone practised together and made all the costumes. All the *paisanas* sewed the outfits and cooked food so that the participants had something to eat during practice. Everyone was proud and wanted to participate and contribute in some form. The strangest thing that nobody can explain is the rain because even though it was not the season, it would always rain that night or the day after the Dragon and the Lion dances. People said that it was the Chinese dances that had made it rain in Tapachula (though I don't believe in things like that), and everyone in town was a witness to this."

Teti "giving life" to the Dragon surrounded by
members of the Chinese community and city
dignitaries (Tapachula's Carnival of 1981).

Spectators cheering after Teti "gives life"
to the Dragon (Tapachula's Carnival of 1981).

One of the many colourful floats participating
in the city's yearly Carnival (mid 1950s).

Listening to Mami, I am transported back to when I was younger and got to enjoy and be part of the same social events. I looked forward to the *piñata* parties, the *sentadas de niño*, the *posadas*, and the cutting of *la rosca de reyes*. Also, I had the opportunity to participate in the city parade when the Chinese community displayed the Dragon and the Lion dances together with a float where some of us girls, dressed in traditional Chinese dresses, would wave to the crowds and throw candies. I even remember reading in the local newspaper about the unexpected rain the day after the Chinese community's ritual dances. But many of these events and parties are not that commonplace anymore because Tapachula has grown larger. Needless to say, I am truly disappointed.

Participating in Tapachula's yearly Carnival. From left:
I, Tío Carlos, Guada, and team performers of the
Dragon Dance and the Lion Dance (1981).

125

A young Mami posing
for a studio portrait
taken in the early 1950s.

11

AN EMPTY HOUSE

AFTER unpacking everything Mami and I bought in the market, I automatically look at the clock on the kitchen wall, where it has always been, and realize it is still early. So I leave Mami in her *oficina* and head to the centre of town to see what changes have occurred since my last visit. I walk by *Long Ying*, an excellent Chinese restaurant owned by Doña Alicia de Chang, one of a small group of Mamita's closest friends, now run by her son Carlos, where the food is excellent. When I was little, the Changs used to live on *la octava* next to the Joos and owned a grocery store. Even though Doña Alicia's children were older, we saw them often. Her youngest son Víctor even rode with us to school for a few years when they lived nearby. Around the time I entered fourth grade, the Changs moved to *la segunda* (Second Avenue) and closer to the *parque*. They opened *Long Ying* and lived in the back part of their establishment, which they still do.

I continue walking by familiar places and discover that some businesses have changed names or are no longer there. On the way back, I stop by to see my godmother

Madrina Chepina, whom I try to see every time I am in town. I say hello briefly to Pei Su, whose real name I do not know; but everyone since I can remember has called him Pei Su, "secretary" in Cantonese. He was the secretary and representative of the Chinese Office in the late 1950s, early 1960s, which looked after the needs and the rights of the Chinese living in Tapachula and nearby areas; the office was also in charge of consular and immigration services. The Chinese population in Tapachula must have been considered significant then for China to establish an official government office. However, most *paisanos* believe that it existed to ensure loyalty to Mainland China rather than to Taiwan. Regardless, the presence of such an office and their representatives was well accepted among the *paisanos* because the office organized community and social events and even sponsored a Chinese-language school for children and youth. Pei Su chose not to return to China after the office closed down and is now very frail but still has an agile mind and a great disposition.

Then I walk two blocks westbound and discover that Don Manuel Chong is not in his fabric store. I am disappointed because I will not have the chance during this trip to return to see him and catch up. His younger children used to participate in a lot of the same community events than my sisters and I did.

Finally, I walk to the other side of town towards the

Instituto Tapachula, a private school run by Catholic nuns, near where Don Pepe Mak and his wife Doña Tere live. I knock on their door but their cleaning lady tells me they are away. Their middle daughter and I have remained pretty close friends in spite of the distance (she lives in Chicago). Both Don Pepe and Doña Tere always welcome me to their home with open arms and give me unusual foods to try. After seeing and talking with everyone, I feel as if I had never left and decide to make it a priority to visit other friends in the days to come.

It is almost 2:00 p.m. and I had promised Mami I would return in time to have *mole de pollo* and *arroz a la mexicana.* While I was growing up, Papito and Mamita always emphasized the importance of being on time for everything, regardless of the occasion. Tardiness, especially being late for a family meal, was not taken very lightly. For both of them, being thirty minutes early was better than being five minutes late. Besides, Mami has to eat like clockwork and cannot deviate much from what she is accustomed to.

This morning, Mami bought some *mole* from a woman down the steep hill who has been making this exquisite sauce from scratch with chocolate, chilies, and plantains for more than twenty years. She still puts a sign outside her garage so people can buy *mole* in plastic bags or order it. She only makes a limited amount every day and sells the last bag quite early in the day. A few days ago when we passed by on our way to the *tortillería*, Mami said she had not had *mole* in a while and had *antojo* (craving).

Since our return from the market, Mami has been cooking an entire chicken. After a few hours, she mixes the *mole* with the broth and adds a few extra chunks of Soconusco chocolate from the area, as she likes her *mole* a bit sweeter. She has cut the chicken and separated out my favourite parts and left hers aside as well. She likes the neck and other pieces that have no meat but, according to her, lots of taste. At the same time, she is also making *arroz a la mexicana* with caramelized onions, rice, fresh tomato puree, chicken broth, and seasonings.

I arrive home in time to heat up the tortillas and set the table. Mami tells me that she needs her chopsticks and her Chinese spoon even though we are having Mexican food. On the centre of the table, there is a plate of fresh avocados seasoned with freshly-squeezed lime juice, salt, and pepper. When we finally sit down at the table, I just smile at her and say, "Mami, *mah-man sek*."

"Years went by and everything was fine," Mami says raising her chopsticks. "I had no idea, but Teti always had a dream of some day returning to China for good with all of us. In preparation for this, he had contacted some of his relatives in Kau Kong and in Hong Kong, and following their advice, he made arrangements with his cousin #4 and his wife to raise our youngest children in a Chinese

From left to right:
Tía Lupe, Tío Juanca, Mami, Tía Chony, Tío Pepe,
Teti's niece Ah-Bun, and one of Ah-Bun's daughters
at Hong Kong International Airport (circa 1959).

environment so they could learn the Chinese language, culture, and customs and be educated in the Chinese tradition. I basically had no say in this, and one day in around 1959, I found myself on a plane with Tía Chony and Tío Pepe, who were eight years old, Tía Lupe who was six years old, and Tío Juanca, aged five, heading to Kowloon. It was a difficult thing to do since I didn't want to in the first place. By this time Papito was twenty-one, had moved from Mexico to Hong Kong, and was continuing his Chinese studies. I met up with Papito and felt so terrible because I left him in charge of his siblings while I returned to Tapachula. It was awful."

With an empty house and no children to look after, Mami began to help out with the store. At first she did not even dare to go downstairs since she did not speak enough Spanish to deal with customers, and she had no real idea what the store was all about. But she slowly gathered the courage and realized it was good for her since it was an opportunity to learn Spanish and also understand how the store ran. Working in it not only made her feel useful, it also made the days go faster and gave her a sense of purpose. The house and her life felt so empty the first years the children were away that she was thankful Teti needed her in the store.

During the nine years that the children were in Kowloon, Mami's life was pretty much routine. She split her time between working in the store and spying on Mincho to learn his cooking techniques. Often she would visit Doña Angela and Tía Chusita, whose children were also away studying. Sometimes the three of them would go to the seamstress to design and get dresses made. Then in the afternoons, she would gossip with the *paisanos* who came to eat and kept her in the loop about what was going on in the community and also in Kau Kong and China. Mami also made sure the house was cleaned and the clothes washed. Then in the afternoons, she would sit together with the maid and watch a couple of soaps; between scenes she would lean over to the maid and ask her what a certain word meant, and with gestures and examples she would acquire a few more Spanish words.

"Every Sunday at around 4:30 a.m., I followed Mincho to the market to learn what to buy and how to bargain. I enjoyed learning how to distinguish what was fresh from what was not, and how by holding the fruits and vegetables, to recognize what was ripe and what was not. After returning, I made and ate breakfast then headed downstairs to help in the store. While Teti and the employees worked as usual on Sunday, I sneaked upstairs around 6:00 p.m. to watch my favourite variety show, *Siempre en Domingo*, with Raúl Velasco, which ran for many, many years."

"Like Doña Angela, Tía Chusita became my good friend. We somehow understood each other even though Tía Chusita did not speak Chinese and my Spanish was worse. But we laughed a lot and cried a lot together, so much that I think we had a solid friendship. When I was still living in Kau Kong, I met Tía Chusita's three children and helped them adapt to a new and strange world in Hong Kong, which I think Tía Chusita was very thankful for. And as soon as I arrived in Tapachula in 1949, Tía Chusita without hesitation helped me to get around and get to know my new surroundings."

Tía Chusita and Mami
(circa 1950).

"Since we lived next to each other, Tía Chusita was always there to take me places, and so she often lent me eggs or whatever Mincho was missing in the kitchen and needed right away. For me it was important that Tía Chusita always kept in mind that since her husband and Teti were related and shared the Lau name, she and I were tied by a special bond and belonged to the same family regardless of whether or not it was by marriage. We grew even closer during the period of time when both our children were away studying."

"Upon returning to Tapachula from their studies in Kau Kong, Tía Nelly, Tía Blanqui, and Ah-Min-Suk stayed with us. Tía Chusita's husband had just passed on so the children came back for good. After almost eleven years in China, they

Mami, Tía Nelly, Tía Chusita, Tía Blanqui, Tío Juanca (circa 1957).

could only speak Chinese and communication between them and their mother was a problem. So Tía Chusita's three children lived for a few months in Casa Lau with Teti and me and the rest of the Chinese employees. That helped the children ease their transition as they slowly re-learned Spanish and got reacquainted with the taste of Mexican food and with a different lifestyle and way of doing things. After about eight months, Tía Nelly, Tía Blanqui, and Ah-Min-Suk returned to live with Tía Chusita."

While Mami goes to watch her soaps, I head back to exploring every single closet and cabinet remaining in the house. This time I leave nothing untouched, except the boxes marked with my aunts' names. I remember that when I was little, I would go into Teti's office behind the store and inspect both of his desks and any dusty box I could find. I discovered many treasures, including old Mexican and Chinese silver coins which I would beg him to allow me to keep.

Now, in my old bedroom, I see tucked behind my wooden desk a framed photo of Teti formally dressed, accepting some sort of certificate and shaking hands with four men in suits who look quite important. With a matching wood frame, I also find the actual certificate given to Teti in August 1965 by the Mexican local and state Chamber of Commerce for twenty-five years of professionalism in the business community. I take the photo and the certificate and clean them carefully. Then, holding onto both I head to the sliding door of the back patio and sit on the green and black ottoman of the living room set.

Mami joins me and looks at what I am holding in my hands. She tells me proudly that this was just one small token of recognition Teti received throughout the years. Aside from the browning of the paper, she is surprised that both items have survived rather well. Reading my thoughts, she tells me to take both frames back with me to Vancouver since there is nobody here to admire and care for them.

We are sitting on the ottoman enjoying the sunset, just as I remember my father Papito doing once in a while. The sky changes in colour from yellow to orange to red then purple and finally to a light blue. With the sun gone, the intense heat dissipates and the temperature goes down ever so slightly. The breeze and fresh air add to the simple enjoyment of each other's company, as we listen to the crowing of a rooster somewhere below us and the sound of a couple of *cuijas*, small, brownish lizards that feel cold to the touch, crawling on the wall somewhere above us.

I turn my head and with a smile ask Mami, *"¿Y sabe cómo llegó Teti por primera vez a Tapachula?"* ("And do you know how Teti arrived for the first time in Tapachula?").

When I was little, I heard on many occasions that Teti arrived in Tapachula after a long and difficult trip by boat. But his plan was to remain in Tapachula for only a few years, just long enough to make enough money for his final destination: San Francisco, in Chinese *Kam San* or Golden Mountain. But having prospered here, he decided to stay on, only returning to Kau Kong many years later to get married. When I had dared to ask why Teti had chosen Tapachula, I would either get different answers or a "young girls do not ask that many questions," comment or a simply "I do not know." I could never really ask such a simple question and get an answer that satisfied me. This time, I do not want to hear the same version I had to memorize and give to strangers. Instead, I am hopeful Mami will tell me more details about Teti's trip and about his life.

"I really never talked much with Teti about his life. The past was the past, and there were things better left unsaid. It was not proper either for me to ask your grandfather about this or about anything he would not voluntarily mention himself. But from the things he said here and there and during the time we were together, I can tell you some things. Mostly, I think your father would know more than I do."

I just smile sweetly at Mami and encourage her to tell me what she knows.

12

AN UNFAMILIAR
DESTINATION

"I think Teti was born in 1900, but I am not sure," Mami answers. "I know that he was born in Kau Kong and left his hometown very young, perhaps when he was around eighteen. He was the eldest son of eight and they were a poor, farming family living in the countryside, where there were no fish, no shrimp, and simply no resources. It was difficult to make ends meet, even for someone like Teti who knew how to write and read. Teti thought that the only way to break this cycle was to get out and make money somewhere else. His goal was not really to become wealthy, but rather to get out of the poverty that had followed many of his ancestors and to be able to have enough to start a family of his own."

"Leaving China was not that simple. Teti needed someone who trusted and believed in him with enough resources to help him out. All the Laus in Kau Kong were related in one way or another, and the distinction was only made on how close or distant this person was to Teti. One of his distant *Ah-Suk* [uncle] wanted to sponsor him to get out of Kau Kong by employing Teti in his trading company. At the time, most trading companies were simple storefronts where anything and everything was sold. These were also where you went if you needed to send, receive, and keep money safely, like a bank nowadays."

"Teti's *Ah-Suk* needed employees not only in Hong Kong but also in other countries where he was expanding or trading. So Teti took the opportunity and went to Hong Kong, where he worked for approximately one year. But, like everyone, he had to start from the bottom and move up, and nobody was allowed to jump ahead. So he began by cleaning the floors in the store, fetching water, making tea, and running errands. Then he got to be the cook's assistant, and finally, though briefly, he got to work in the store. When he arrived in Hong Kong, Teti realized quickly that living and working conditions were tough and very similar to anywhere else in China. So the real solution was to get to *Kam San*, San Francisco, where stories about success and riches were making their way back to China and Hong Kong."

"Just like one had to do their time and move from one task to the next, there was also a waiting period and a list where a person had to put his name if he wanted to leave Hong Kong to work in Southeast Asia or San Francisco. Teti put his name on the list and waited and waited for what seemed to him a long time. He persevered and decided to ask his boss every day when he would be the next person to leave. He knew his work was good, but he just needed a chance. Although it was not Teti's turn, one day his boss finally came to him and said that there was a spot in Mexico. His incessant asking had paid off, but Teti had no idea where Mexico was or where in Mexico he was going. It didn't matter. He accepted the job because he thought (or perhaps convinced himself) that things in Mexico couldn't be worse than in China or Hong Kong."

I only learned recently, while doing research for my master's thesis, that Mexico had a notable immigration from China in the late 1800s as a consequence of economic turmoil, famine, drought, and political uncertainty. Coincidentally, Porfirio Díaz, the dictator of Mexico at the time, was looking for a way to populate and develop the desert lands of northern Mexico, mainly states such as Baja California, Sonora, Chihuahua, Sinaloa, and Coahuila. By signing a treaty with China, Díaz negotiated the emigration of a significant number of male Chinese labourers to Mexico from the late 1800s through the early 1900s. These groups of Chinese migrants were part of a larger wave of emigration from China in the nineteenth century. Though most Chinese looked to Southeast Asia, and later North America, for refuge, a smaller but still significant number of emigrants headed to Latin America: Peru, Cuba, and Mexico. In the case of Mexico, most Chinese labourers were assigned to the northern states to work the land and assist in construction of the railroad. While some of these workers eventually settled in the northern states (continuing

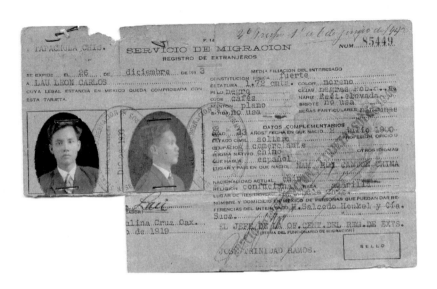

Teti's immigration card found in a cardboard box
at the National Archives in Mexico City.

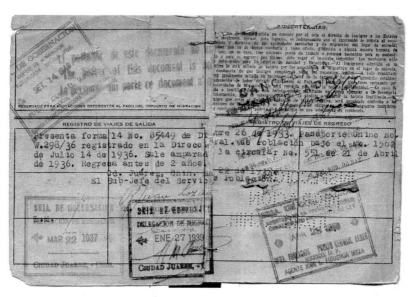

to work the land), others went north to the United States, returned to China, or headed to other parts of Mexico.

The Chinese who chose to stay in Mexico eventually sought other opportunities and became successful entrepreneurs by establishing small shops and creating a business network. Some eventually sponsored other Chinese to work in their businesses as either partners or employees. But during the Mexican Revolution of 1911, the Chinese (especially those who had become successful businessmen) were violently persecuted, resulting in most of them being deported and stripped of their businesses and property. At that time, a small number of Chinese headed south to areas where the internal unrest was less violent and the aggression was not directed towards them or their property. By the time the violent phase of the Mexican Revolution ended in 1921, the Chinese population had dramatically dwindled, especially in the northern states where their presence, in previous decades, had been felt the most.

Some Chinese who headed to the less tumultuous southern areas must have ended up in Tapachula and surrounding areas in the state of Chiapas. They most likely became part of an already well-established Chinese community. But how the first Chinese arrived in this southern and remote part of Mexico, how they established this community, and how they led their lives remains a mystery. It is left to speculation, even now among the Chinese in Tapachula, whether this community was comprised of men who had finished working on construction of the Panama Canal, or been brought in to build the southern railroad, or been sent by Chinese businessmen who had expanded their commercial ventures into this part of the country, or for some other reason.

As I listen to Mami, I reflect on how it must have been for Teti to arrive in Mexico in 1919 at the age of nineteen with only a few coins in his pocket and speaking only *Kau Kong Wah*. According to his immigration / registration card issued by the *Secretaría de Migración* in 1933, which I found in the *Archivo General de la Nación* (the National Archives, in Mexico City), he came by boat and entered through the port of Salina Cruz in Oaxaca. During this forty-day journey, he travelled from Hong Kong to Japan to Hawaii then to San Francisco (interestingly enough), and finally to Mexico. Although it was a harsh, arduous long trip that many men did not survive, I do not recall Teti ever talking about it.

"The entire trip," Mami continues with a sombre look, "was done in an enclosed and small area where disease, dirt, human waste, and death were the norm; it certainly was no cruise ship. From the port of Salina Cruz, Teti rode 430 kilometres east to Tapachula on the back of a *carreta* [a horse or ox-drawn open-air carriage], which was simply a few planks of wood put together like a roof-less trailer large enough to carry supplies. There were no clearly marked roads at the time, only dusty, bumpy, narrow trails where people walked and horses, mules, and *carretas* trotted between *fincas* and towns."

"As soon as he arrived, Teti began working in his Ah-Suk's store as an employee. His Ah-Suk was Tía Nelly's oldest paternal uncle, who had an established storefront that allowed him to bring over, one by one, all of his brothers and cousins from China. It took Teti about five years to repay the debts for his trip to Mexico, and eventually he was able to open his own *tienda de abarrotes* (a neighbourhood grocery store) in another part of town, much smaller than his Ah-Suk's store."

"Because he was friendly, funny, and easy-going, Teti quickly became friends with both *tapachultecos* and Chinese. And mostly because of his integrity, honesty, trustworthiness, and strong work ethic, many of them entrusted him with the money and merchandise to start Casa Lau. I don't think nowadays anybody helps you like they helped Teti out."

Although it had officially been a city since the mid-1800s, by the time Teti arrived in 1919, Tapachula had a population of no more than 20,000. It was charming and small with dusty roads and only a few cobblestone streets. The houses were quite rustic, built with long-lasting materials and designed for comfort and ventilation against the high humidity and the heat. Some houses were made of *adobe* (stone, mud, and straw) and some of *otate* (very strong cane sticks) with either *teja* (clay tiles), palm leaves, or tin roofing.

AN UNFAMILIAR DESTINATION

Teti opened Casa Lau in a small building with *teja* roofing on the northwest edge of town in the old neighbourhood called *barrio de San Juan*. This area was located on the city limits on *la octava* or 8th Avenue, which connected to a road to *Nueva Alemania* and other important *fincas* that produced coffee beans. At first, Teti rented this building. Years later, as the business grew, he bought it outright from the Aceves, a well-known family in Tapachula even today. Through different periods of growth a few additions, possible only at the back or on top, were made to the main building and, as in any business, employees came and went.

"By the time Papito and I arrived in Tapachula in 1949," Mami continues, "Casa Lau was well-established with steady customers in spite of two bankruptcies and countless problems throughout the years [like not having enough money to buy merchandise, customers not wanting to pay their debts, eating the losses of merchandise that got spoiled because of the humidity, heat, or bugs]. The store had a few long wooden counters piled high with goods also reaching the ceiling on wooden shelves."

"At first, Casa Lau sold mostly canned foods and dry goods, cigarettes, candies, and cookies in small quantities. Then Teti began buying products in bigger stores for resale in Casa Lau. Most goods such as sugar, salt, flour, rice, and black beans came in fifty-kilogram sacks. Even cookies and candies came in large packages. So the employees would repack these

147

goods into smaller bags so families in the neighbourhood could buy what they needed in the amounts they wanted."

I remember spending many afternoons as a little girl weighing sugar into one-kilogram paper bags and carefully folding the edges or placing 100 grams of animal cookies in plastic bags and sealing them by folding the open end against the teeth of a sawblade and melting this part of the plastic bag by passing it quickly near a candle flame. Just to make it a fun activity, Teti would start competitions to see who was faster, but he always beat every employee who considered himself fast, and folded bags better than anybody else.

As the business grew, Teti started to buy from main suppliers and manufacturers, and began to sell wholesale as well. Casa Lau was not only selling to families in the neighbourhood but also to the *fincas, ranchos,* and corner stores. The inventory was varied in that it included blankets, clothing, *sombreros,* pots and pans, toiletries and toilet paper, over-the-counter medicine like alka seltzer for indigestion and *mejoral* for colds, and everything else needed in any household, including oil lamps and manual grinders called *molinos* to grind the maize for tortillas. Casa Lau also sold construction materials such as sheets of tin roofing, tools like hammers and saws, nails, and products needed in the *fincas* (from smaller machinery to industrial sizes, such as larger *molinos* for both coffee and maize, tools used in the fields such as hoes, shovels, pails, and even ropes in all lengths and in all thickness). There were also miscellaneous items, like batteries and school supplies, notebooks, pens, pencils, compasses, rulers, and different colours of papier maché, wrapping paper, and rice paper. Casa Lau had everything needed to do all the shopping in one stop. Even when I was growing up, the store had most of these items for sale.

For customers who made big purchases, their products were placed inside cardboard boxes (recycled from merchandise that the store had bought wholesale) and tied neatly with thin but strong cord made of *henequén* (sisal). This way of repackaging helped safely transport goods over long and bumpy roads back to the *fincas* in the mountains. Most customers who made small purchases carried with them recyclable and durable bags. If they did not have bags, their products were placed into small boxes or wrapped with newspaper. This is the way most, if not all such stores, handled their sold goods.

Next to the grocery store, Teti had opened a small *cantina* (bar) with a few tables and chairs where alcohol was served. It had a different entrance, and there was a wall between the store and the *cantina*. It was a loud place and fights sometimes ensued. Because of the headache of running such a place, Papito closed it down after we were born and converted it into much needed warehouse space. Even so, the *cantina* had remained in business for nearly thirty years.

"When Teti began Casa Lau," Mami tells me, "he worked

alone and did everything himself. Shortly after he had a few employees, Mexican and Chinese men. Most of the Chinese men were Teti's nephews he had sponsored from Kau Kong to work in the store. But Teti also employed other Chinese men who were either relatives or friends. Casa Lau was open from 5:00 a.m. until 10:00 p.m. every day, but actually it was open 24 hours, 7 days a week, 365 days all year round. There was a small wooden window on the side of the store where customers could make their purchases, and Teti would get up in the middle of the night or whenever there was a knock on the window. Most times, it was a customer who had run out of kerosene for his lamp and was in dire need of it."

"In the beginning, Teti and his nephews worked and lived in the store. At night, they would clean the counters, spread some newspapers over and use them as beds to sleep. They had their meals on the counters or sat somewhere in the store for some quiet time since it didn't close down throughout the day. Everyone was responsible for attending to the customers and keeping the store clean and well-stocked. As Casa Lau expanded and the warehouse was built, the part of it behind the store was used as living quarters by Teti and his employees. Eventually, the back of the store was completely converted into living space, and the two floors below, following the curve of the hill, were built to store more goods."

I realize it is late already and that Mami needs to go to bed soon.

Mami (second from the left), Teti (in glasses),
their children, nephews, and employees
in Casa Lau (circa 1957).

"It was a long time ago since I watched a sunset. I am a little cold now with this night breeze," Mami says. "But it is nice to sit in our living room."

I get up to close the sliding door and head to the kitchen to get some fruit. I know I will not be able to sleep on an empty stomach. Mami follows me and after I peel a couple of oranges, I hand her a few wedges.

"Are the oranges sweet and juicy?" Mami asks me before taking any. "You know that I don't like to eat fruits unless they are very sweet. *Ngo hou soi* [I am very bad]. So try them first and only give me a few pieces if they are sweet."

I curl my lips and twist my face after eating a wedge. "*Kong siu, Ah-Mami* [I'm just kidding, Mami]. The oranges are very sweet." She laughs and reaches for a few wedges and jokingly swears at me, "Cabrona."

After we finish eating, Mami goes to the bathroom and gets ready for bed.

"Tomorrow, Tío Carlos is driving us out to Cacahuatán, and we'll be out most of the day," Mami reminds me. "So go to bed early."

"Don't worry, Mami, I remember. I'll close the doors and windows and go to bed soon. *Chou tau*, Mami," I respond.

13

TETI

TÍO Carlos is a certified public accountant with a large office in the centre of town. But he is also a professor in auditing at UNACH, Chiapas State University, teaching every afternoon for over twenty years and still loving every minute. Since today is Sunday, however, he does not need to go to his office to work or to the university to teach. Instead, he and Tía Elda pick Mami and me up to go to nearby Cacahuatán for their famous *carne asada* for lunch. When we were children, we used to go to Unión Juarez for this delicious meat barbecue. But Tía Elda tells me that now Cacahuatán is where everybody goes since the beef is excellent, and they still make their tortillas by hand and cook them on an open fire.

On the way, we stop by the *panteón* and instead of fresh flowers, opt to light some candles on the gravestones of Teti, Tío Pepe, my sister Angelita, and Mami's nephew, Ramón. Mami is afraid that this time, since we are in Tapachula only for a visit, we will not be able to return to remove the dead flowers before we leave town.

After leaving Tapachula, we drive for half an hour along a green and lush, winding road, leading to the town of Cacahuatán. We pass by a few streets with small, tin-roofed houses painted in bright colours, and see trees full of *carambolas* (star fruit) and gardens with bright pink bougainvilleas. Then we park on the side of the road in front of an open-air restaurant that looks rustic but charming with non-matching rusty metal chairs and tables on an uneven clay floor under a palm-straw roof.

We are welcomed effusively because Tío Carlos seems to know everybody everywhere we go. Then, we sit down and order a cold *Coronita*. Meanwhile, I see a man going back and forth between the open charcoal grill (where he is cooking thin slices of marinated beef) and a wooden stove (where he is cooking *caldo de frijol* or black bean soup). Also, I see a woman very adeptly and quickly tapping small chunks of corn flour dough and shaping each individually into a perfectly round tortilla, then placing each on a flat, metal griddle covered with white limestone powder called a *comal* which lies on top of a wood open fire pit. Tío Carlos tells me that if I like tripe and "all that good stuff," this is the place to enjoy them. Tía Elda just rolls her eyes and says she will only have beef.

After eating and before leaving Cacahuatán, Tía Elda suggests that, since we have driven so far, we should stop by a grocery store owned by a *paisano* who makes Chinese pastries.

We park in front of the market and walk the bustling main street to the *tienda de abarrotes*, busy with customers on a late Sunday afternoon. Tía Elda buys a few crusty pastries filled with sweet *tou sah* for her Mom (who has grown to like them), for Mami, and a couple more for dinner since she will not cook after such a large lunch.

On our way back to Tapachula, we open the windows and enjoy the smell of the jungle and the humidity. Tía Elda takes out one of the Chinese pastries and shares it with Mami and me. It is quite good, but Tía Elda says that the sweet bean paste is not as moist as Mami's.

Mami, of course, gives me a smile and replies, *"¿De a de veras, Elda?"* ("Truly, Elda?"). In reality she wants to hear more compliments about her cooking. Tío Carlos just laughs, shakes his head, and drops us off at Casa Lau. He is in a hurry to get home to watch the customary Sunday soccer matches on TV.

Mami decides she wants to organize a Chinese lunch at Tía Nelly's *Kam Long* for next week and begins to call a few people. It is late in the afternoon, and I am going down the yellow staircase to the area where we stored sacks of sugar. When Casa Lau was in business, there were stacks of empty boxes underneath the staircase and all over this area. When we were children, we would unpack merchandise to be put on the shelves, leaving the empty boxes here because they were bulky. One of our favourite games was to spread out as many empty cardboard boxes as we could to build houses to live in. Very often, the houses would be transformed into stores, and we would play *a la tiendita*, where we bought, sold, and bargained over our stuffed animals and imaginary toys in exchange for monopoly money.

When I reach this lower part of the house, I see resurfaced walls where three different doors used to be: one door led to the store and two others to warehouses. I realize how fortunate we were in having not only empty boxes to play with, but also large places to hide, climb, jump, and hunt for treasures and live, black bats. When we were growing up, our "playground" used to be quite extensive. Along with Tía Nelly's three children and Tía Blanqui's three, my sisters and I (all nine of us) played in the three families' warehouses. Located side by side, we would cross back and forth between Tía Nelly's and Tía Blanqui's houses, which were connected at the top level on the *azotea* and at the bottom through their separate warehouses. When we got tired of playing in these warehouses, we would go across the steep street to Casa Lau and sneak into that warehouse to continue playing. In spite of our parents' constant admonitions and warnings that warehouses were dangerous and unsuitable for children, we spent a considerable time playing in these dark, cool mazes, stacked high with merchandise, avoiding getting caught by any means possible. I feel a knot in my stomach as I realize I cannot access these areas anymore. Perhaps it is silly, but I would like just one chance to walk through these meaningful places.

When I am at the bottom of the staircase, Mami's voice brings me back to the present. I hear her asking me what I am doing and the sound of her footsteps following me down. She stops halfway and sits down on one of the steps. I tell her I am simply going to a panel where the electric fuses for the main floor and the switch for the main holding tank are located.

Before we run out of water, I turn on the pump to refill the main holding tank. By replenishing it now, we will have enough water during the times of the day that the city water supply is shut off. The main holding tank was built in the back bottom patio, and it is very large (approximately thirty feet long by 13 feet wide and at least 7 feet high).

I remember where the switch is since I took turns with Mamita to turn it on almost every day for a few hours and then off again. If either of us forgot to turn it on, somebody would end up without water in the middle of a shower. If we neglected to turn it off after a while, whoever happened to be upstairs in the house would hear the water overflowing.

I head back up stairs to join Mami, and we sit on the steps and chat.

"When Teti arrived, the Chinese community in Tapachula was quite large. From what Teti said, the population stayed steady between 350 to 400 Chinese men in the 1920s and 1930s, and even perhaps in the 1940s. One time, it even reached as high as 600 men. Many came from China through

Central America or from the northern states of Mexico; for instance, Don Panchito's father had come from Zacatecas somewhere north, and Doña Susana's family were from Manzanillo."

Sometimes when Teti reminisced about the good old times, he talked about the many teahouses and small Chinese restaurants that Tapachula had where men could gather or stop by to chat. He also mentioned stories with names that Mami would not recognize about such and such *paisano* who had returned to China or had passed away here, never to return home.

Teti talked about the lavish banquets which featured expensive abalone, shark's fin, or bird's nest soup and hard-to-find dried mushrooms that many of the men who owned the larger trading companies had in their homes. The dishes were even made using real soy sauce shipped in small glass bottles from China and not the cheap imitation brand that came in twenty-litre cans. Many of these men invited their Mexican friends who had become wealthy ranchers and business people and even polititians. It became fashionable to be invited as a guest to these banquets, especially if you were a Mexican. This way, many locals learned to enjoy Chinese food and befriended the *paisanos*. When I was young, even though the number of Chinese had dwindled, I would see Teti going out to his customary Tuesday night dinners with the elders in the community. He would dress up in his long-sleeved *guayabera* shirt and dark pants, wear his gold watch and splash on some Old Spice for such a special event, just like he did when he went to his monthly Board of Directors' meetings at the bank.

Teti's life was Casa Lau, and what made Casa Lau full of life and gave importance to the Lau last name was Teti. Though he worked hard and long hours, he spent all his time at the store doing something he loved and was good at, and it was not what he would have considered "work." He knew by name almost every customer who walked in the door. Being self-motivated, he taught himself to speak, write, and read in Spanish. He also learned, by repetition, enough words to do business in *chamula*, enough to make somebody feel welcome, and in other languages spoken by indigenous people in the surrounding areas.

In his own naïveté, Teti believed in the goodness of people and gave credit to anybody who would ask for it. He trusted relatives and employees as well, which almost led to his downfall because he nearly lost Casa Lau twice when he left the store in his nephews' care and went to China. Numerous outstanding unpaid bills were never settled. And since relatives and employees working at the store had open access to the till, there was no real account or control of the store's cash sales. Therefore Casa Lau was in constant financial trouble under Teti's command.

Teti loved his abacus. He rarely used a calculator, an

adding machine, and was even against getting a cash register for the store. He always kept his old wooden abacus within reach and was the fastest person to do math calculations no matter how long or complicated they were. Teti's fingers would gracefully and quickly fly up and down the black round beads and only stop when he blurted out the final answer. I remember employees challenging him to a match of speed and precision: Teti with his abacus, one employee with a calculator, and another one with an adding machine. And in front of customers Teti would show everyone over and over how much faster and without mistakes he could add, subtract, multiply, and divide with his abacus over anybody who used the latest technology. Now I so wish I had paid attention when Teti was trying to teach me how to use his abacus when I was younger.

Before Mami and Papito bought a new cash register that helped track the taxes on different items, Teti kept bills in a locked drawer and later used an old bulky register with number keys that would not stay down when you pushed them. For loose change and coins, an old wooden box with three compartments was used, which was placed behind the counter out of the reach of the public. Teti liked to keep things simple, which worked for him.

Eventually, when Mamita and Papito took over more responsibilities at Casa Lau, they purchased a cash register and decided that one person had to always man it in order to keep the business under control. Though at first Teti perceived these practices as unnecessary and rigid, he became convinced that they were effective. So either Mamita or Papito, and eventually one of us daughters, had to always be the cashier and at the same time be in charge of overseeing the employees to make sure customers were being served in a timely manner, and that the right amount of and correct merchandise was leaving the store. Though the old register went out the door, Teti's wooden box for coins behind the cashier's high chair remained in use for as long as I can remember.

Teti loved to be around people. He always had a smile and a sparkle in his eyes and would sing Chinese high-pitched songs all day and affectionately address people as *mashkut* or *huachijul*. If you were a kid, he would call you *mashkutín*, poke your cheeks, and mess up your hair. He joked with friends, customers, and employees alike, always telling stories and making people laugh. When employees were standing around doing nothing, he would walk into the middle of them and "let a few out" while telling them (with a smile) that there were products to be re-stocked or storage room floors to be cleaned if they were bored. The employees would laugh and at the same time express their disgust shaking their heads with an "*órale* (come on), *Don Carlos*," hold their noses, use their remaining hand to fan away the smell, and get back to work.

While we are on this subject, Mami asks me what I remember about Teti, and I tell her I idolized him because I always felt I was his favourite among us three girls. But the truth is that he was a man who was content with simple things and was happy to make everyone feel special, not just me. Teti's favourite pastime was to watch boxing matches on TV. He never watched TV regularly, but when there was a boxing match on, he would simply stand in front of the set and block everyone from watching. Then since nobody at home liked boxing, we would leave the living room and he would comfortably sit down in an armchair and enjoy the fight all by himself.

Mami reminds me that Teti used to ask us three granddaughters to give him a daily massage while he read his Chinese newspaper. He would have Guada take one leg, and me the other, while Vero would be in charge of Teti's shoulders. Then with both our hands clasped in fists, we would pound the part that was allocated to us, being careful not to miss any area. First, we would start softly, as he had shown us how it should be done. With our impatience growing as minutes went by, we would then pound very hard to the point that he would have to yell for us to stop. And the next day, without any exceptions, we would go over the same drill again.

Teti's most memorable moments were when the entire family gathered for a meal or to celebrate something special.

Christmas and New Year's were festive occasions when Mami would spend entire days prior cooking her most delectable dishes, such as stuffed pork roast or her version of chicken à l'orange with *min-si*, Chinese fermented soybeans and orange juice. She would also prepare both Mexican *tamales* with maize and chicken in *mole* sauce and Chinese *tamales* with sticky rice and salted eggs. Casa Lau would close down earlier on both Christmas and New Year's eves. Everyone would come for dinner at 8:00 p.m. and stay until 1:00 a.m. or 2:00 a.m. At 12:00 midnight, everyone would hug each other, red Chinese envelopes would be given out to the children, champagne would be served, and all of us children would run to the Christmas tree and open presents. Teti, Papito, and my uncles would go to the front patio and light up long sheets of firecrackers for at least twenty minutes, joining the entire city with festive sounds and fireworks.

Another of Teti's favourite celebrations in Casa Lau was Chinese New Year's. The entire family would come home to eat Mami's raw fish dish with thinly cut vegetables and black bean sauce, lettuce wraps with *hoi sin* sauce, radish cakes, sticky rice *tamales* stuffed with sweet bean paste, and sweet steamed buns or water chestnut cakes as dessert. Once again, the children would anxiously wait for the red envelopes. The adults would enjoy good food, conversation and lots of rum and coke, whiskey and soda water, and cognac.

Mami and I smile remembering one particular family

gathering. It was December 28th *día de los inocentes*, equivalent to the North American April Fools' Day. It had fallen on a Sunday when Casa Lau was closed for the afternoon. With the excuse of celebrating this special day and my uncle Tío Neto and his wife Tía Vicky's wedding anniversary, everyone came to Casa Lau for Mami's family lunch. After eating, Teti was tired and decided to take a few hours for a nap and for some quiet time to read his Chinese newspaper. The afternoon went by and when Teti came back to the dining room, he noticed that lunch had extended to dinner so he rejoined the party. Quickly, he realized that all his sons and sons-in-laws had had too much to drink. Almost a case of

From left: Tía Lupe, Teti, Mami, and Tía Chony at home on top of Casa Lau before leaving to Hotel Kamico for a party celebration of Teti's 80th birthday (1980).

twelve bottles of hard liquor had been digested in barely six hours, in addition to beer and other alcoholic drinks. As the father figure, Teti got up and harshly scolded them one by one, sending everyone home. That night, Mami told Teti that there had been no need to spoil the party since the "children" were just having fun, daydreaming about some nonsense of a family car trip that would take a few months through the jungle northbound to Cancun and back. With a big smile, Teti replied that he had had to show he was the head of the family by acting somewhat sternly, but the truth was he was dying to sit down and have a drink of whiskey with his stinky and noisy "children."

From left: Mamita, Teti, Mami, and Papito.

Remembering these times, Mami tells me again that she had been very fortunate marrying Teti. He always took care of her and respected her. They did not know each other at first but grew to like and appreciate each other with time. Teti's priorities were the family and Casa Lau. He did not smoke or drink or gamble. He just liked to play *tin kau*, some sort of Chinese dominos, but only for fun. So Teti was the best husband she could have asked for.

Teti playing tin kau during a visit to Ah-Bun's in New York City (mid 1970s).

14

UNFORESEEN CIRCUMSTANCES

MAMI and I are sitting with a cup of *Soconusco* coffee (mine more like a cup of milk with a touch of coffee just like when I was a kid) and a plate full of *tortitas de plátano*, which she bought from a vendor passing by. We used to buy these at school (also from a street vendor) during recess as a snack or sometimes even a meal. They are mashed plantains deep-fried and sugar-coated, shaped like an elongated egg with a refried-black-bean centre. I tell Mami I had not had one of these delicious *tortitas* in a long time, and she insists I should eat them all. But I do not think I can eat all eight at once, especially if I do not want to suffer from a bad case of constipation.

At home we used to eat *platanitos fritos*, perhaps because they were healthier and easier to make than the *tortitas*. Mami would cut the plantains when they were soft to the touch and the skin was totally black; then she fried them in very little oil and served them. They were so sweet and tasty they would be gone in no time. When I ate at friends' and neighbours' homes, they served fried plantains with fresh, thick cream and salty, crumbly local cheese, which was the traditional way.

While we eat, Mami tells me that around 1965, Teti was thinking about joining their children in Kowloon for good. "Papito had his own apartment and was already working for a high-end clothing store in the accounting department in Hong Kong; and best of all, he had been married for two years to a Chinese girl. Tía Chony, Tío Pepe, Tía Lupe, and Tío Juanca were doing well at school and becoming very Chinese in their ways. Teti was in communication with Papito and had announced a plan to sell or close down Casa Lau. Another idea was to leave Casa Lau to somebody Teti trusted to manage it, but he was least excited about this

At my parents' wedding in Kowloon in 1963.
From left: Ah-Popo, Mamita, Mami, and guests.

168

option from past bad experiences. Then we would join the family in Kowloon or return to our house in Kau Kong, and open another business."

"But in his letters, Papito replied that the economic situation in Asia, especially in Hong Kong and in Kau Kong, was not very prosperous. Overall, it was difficult to make ends meet. On the other hand, the situation in Mexico was stable and very positive, and though Casa Lau was in financial disarray, the family was not going to go hungry and could survive if they were thrifty. Without Casa Lau, Teti and Papito reached the conclusion that things would be more difficult, especially if Teti had to start another business all over again or if he decided to leave the store to somebody else to manage."

"In addition, Tío Pepe, Tía Chony, Tía Lupe, and Tío Juanca were still young and needed many more years of schooling before being able to get jobs. After much thought, Papito suggested that he would return to Tapachula with his new wife to help Teti take care of the store."

As the oldest son, Papito took responsibility but he had a lot to lose from his decision to come back and tie his life to Casa Lau. Teti was sixty-five years old, and though he had a few more years to put into the business, he could not realistically continue with the store all by himself. Teti also knew that he was terribly indebted and needed Papito's help to pull Casa Lau out their bad financial situation. Though

Papito never mentioned anything at that time, both Teti and Mami later found out that Papito had declined a job offer to work for Cathay Pacific and that my mother and he were giving up a lot more than just a lifestyle to come to Tapachula and look after the business. But Teti and Mami had no other choice and were truthfully delighted and relieved that Papito was eventually to take over full responsibilities for Casa Lau. And I am left to wonder if Papito thinks at all about this crossroad in his life.

So, Papito and Mamita (pregnant with Guada) left Hong Kong and arrived in Tapachula in 1966. Papito was around twenty-nine and Mamita was twenty-two years old. She had never been in Mexico and spoke no Spanish. They settled in a small bedroom at the back of the store on top of the warehouse, where Mami and Teti were already living. Meanwhile, Tío Pepe, Tía Chony, Tía Lupe, and Tío Juanca remained in Kowloon to continue their studies. Their uncle and aunt #4 accepted full responsibility for looking after them.

By 1967, Mao's Cultural Revolution was making everyone nervous all over the world, especially those who worried about their loved ones in China and in Hong Kong including Teti, Mami, and Papito. It was too risky and worrisome to have the children in Kowloon under the circumstances. So, following the advice of relatives who were living closer to the revolution, Teti and Papito decided to have the children

Photo sent to Mami and Teti in Tapachula
showing their children well taken care of
by their aunt #4 and other relatives
a year after their arrival in Kowloon (circa 1960).

return to Tapachula, which they did around the beginning of 1968. In all those nine years, Mami had only visited her children twice in Hong Kong, so she silently rejoiced to know that she would have them back soon. Having them back was one of Mami's happiest and most memorable moments in her life.

In the end, this had been a difficult decision for Teti. It had taken so much effort and resources to send and keep the children in Hong Kong, and he was glad to know that they were already getting used to the Chinese way of living. In his mind, he had planned they would stay, eventually marry, and reunite when Mami and he returned to Kau Kong. On the other hand, he wanted his children to be safe and would not leave such things to chance a second time in his life. Thus he opted to postpone his dreams of one day returning to live for good with his family in China.

"When Papito returned from Hong Kong," Mami says, "I felt I didn't need to spend so much time in the store. I was looking forward to the birth of my first grandchild. So I stopped altogether helping out in the store and focused on taking care of the home and spying more on Mincho to learn his little cooking tricks."

One and a half years later, Mami had a full house when my aunts and uncles returned to Tapachula. She devoted most of her attention to her children, feeling she needed to make up for lost time. They were now living at home and attending secondary school. Mami spent her energy also caring for Guada and was excited about the birth of her second grandchild, me. Mami says that life was as any normal family would have it.

Almost two years after Guada was born, I arrived on an early afternoon in April 1968, in the same quiet hospital where most children in Tapachula were born, called *Sanatorio Lourdes*. Like most Mexicans, I was named after my mother. Mamita became Rebecca *grande* and I was Rebeca *chica*. Our names were spelled differently because my mother's is the anglicized version from her personal documents issued in Hong Kong (a British colony at the time) and mine is the Spanish version. Up to this day, Mamita reminds me how useless her efforts had been to convince the clerk at the government registration office in Tapachula to spell my name "properly" with two c's.

At the time, Mamita always questioned why everybody in Mexico had to be named the same in one family. It was confusing to call our house and ask for "Carlos" since at one point there were six members of our family named "Carlos." To make matters worse, out of these six, five were "Carlos Lau." So the caller had to state if he was looking for Carlos the accountant or Carlos the engineer, or say the full name, such as Carlos Luis or Juan Carlos.

"One sunny afternoon in July (a few months after you were born), we were all gathered around the large round dining table in the back of the store. By then, Casa Lau [like all businesses] was closed between 2:00 p.m. and 4:00 p.m. for lunch and siesta time. Everyone except Tío Pepe was present, chatting and eating. That day, Tío Pepe was out at a school trip about a couple hours away. Suddenly one black butterfly came out of nowhere and without hesitation stood on Teti's nose. Everyone commented about it and continued eating. I can still remember that butterfly."

"At the same time, Tío Pepe and his friends and classmates were enjoying themselves at the side of a lagoon next to a set of waterfalls. It was an idyllic place to spend a warm afternoon having lunch and splashing in the water. Suddenly, they all turned to see somebody in the water calling for help. Tío Pepe was slim and in good shape, and witnesses say that without thinking he went into the water to rescue this person. Minutes later in what seemed an eternity, he appeared pushing this person out. Everyone was delighted, but that didn't last long because [for some unknown reason] Tío Pepe was pulled down in a flash."

"We didn't know anything until hours later when someone came running into Casa Lau with news that Tío Pepe had disappeared into the water. The rest happened in slow motion as if my whole life had suddenly stopped. Teti and Papito immediately went to the lagoon, and I stayed behind in a total state of disbelief. What the rest of the family did, I couldn't care less. As it was getting dark, nobody was allowed to get into the water and risk somebody else's life. So we waited and waited for what it seemed an eternity. Whatever happened and was said that night is very fuzzy."

"The following day, rescuers went into the water. After much searching, they found Tío Pepe stuck in some rocks underwater with an expression of innocence and peacefulness. He was kneeling with his hands softly holding onto his heart and the cross that hung from his neck placed in his mouth. I wanted to know this much. I was in such a state of shock that I couldn't bring myself together to go to where I had lost Tío Pepe. I don't think I have ever talked with anybody about what happened to him that day or about him when he was alive without feeling an ache in my chest. He was one month short of reaching his seventeenth birthday."

With tears in her eyes and a tissue in her right, Mami is barely able to say any more. "Though he died saving somebody else's life, neither Teti nor I ever really got over his young death." Mami gazes at the floor, shaking her head, and barely whispers, "It is unnatural and out of synch for a child to die before a parent."

Tío Pepe, Mami, Tío Juanca celebrating
Mother's Day (around 1958).

15

CROSSROADS

TODAY we are having lunch at Tía Nelly's *Kam Long* restaurant. Since we are leaving Tapachula in a couple of days, Mami wants to have a thank-you and good-bye party. So she invites Tío Carlos, Tía Elda, Tío Neto, Tía Vicky, Doña Julia, and a couple of Tía Lupe's friends. We also ask Tía Nelly, Ka-Yeh, and my cousin Ani to sit with us in between serving their customers.

Both Mami and I are looking forward to some delicious short ribs, one of the restaurant's signature dishes. We get a private airconditioned room with a bell we can push if we need anything. Mami has preordered the usual: *kai teng, chop suey, chow mein*, fried rice, and deep-fried *wonton* with sweet and sour dipping sauce, fried chicken in soy sauce, in addition to the short ribs. We ask Tía Nelly to make a couple of additional dishes for take-out for Tía Vicky since she has to leave early to get to work and for her mother Doña Julia, who is not feeling very well and is home resting.

It seems everyone is having a good time chatting, laughing, eating, and drinking. All the dishes are gone in no time, but of course the bottles of *Coronitas* keep coming, and Mami insists on ordering more in spite of everyone's protests that they all have had more than their share. Luckily we are in an enclosed room since everyone is getting louder and louder with each drink.

Three hours later, we all kiss each other good-bye with promises to see one another soon. After everyone leaves, Mami pays Tía Nelly a bit more than what has been written on the bill since Mami knows Tía Nelly is giving her an unnecessary and unrequested discount. And as Mami says, "Business is business."

After talking with Tía Nelly and Ka-Yeh, we head home slowly crossing *la octava* and thinking with much dread that our plane leaves in just two more days. As soon as we have entered our silver *portón* and climbed the yellow staircase, Mami mentions that she would like to begin closing Casa Lau up. So, we place all the unopened cans of foods and unsealed packages of crackers and cookies on the shelves so they can be eaten next time by whoever comes to stay. But in the midst of this, Mami stops and asks me to sit down for a minute. She seems anxious to tell me something important. So I sit down next to her at our kitchen table.

"Shortly before leaving for Mexico in 1949, both Teti and I were very busy packing and trying to get money for our trip. It was already a stressful time and to add to this, I was pregnant and not feeling all that great. But just a few days before our departure, Teti pulled me aside with a serious look on his face and confessed to me that during the war, when communication was interrupted and Teti had no idea whether Papito and I were dead or alive, he had had two small sons [Tío Neto and Tío Carlos] in Tapachula with a Mexican woman named Doña Carmen. It had been a brief relationship, and the boys were living with their mother. That was all that was said, and I didn't ask any questions. At that moment, I was uncertain about going to Mexico with him. I had a son and a house in Kau Kong, and I had survived the war all by myself. After all, I knew in my heart I could manage on my own and needed no one else's help. I really didn't need to go anywhere. I cried and cried and no clear solution came to mind. But in the end, I felt I had no other choice and, after many tears, decided to follow Teti to an unknown and distant place on the other side of the world."

More than fifty years later, Mami sits in front of me saying with certain regret, "If this had happened today, I would have seen that I did have a choice."

I hold Mami's hand, trying to comfort her.

"When Tío Neto and Tío Carlos learned that their half-brother Pepe had drowned," Mami explains, "they decided to interrupt their studies in Mexico City and head back to Tapachula. They were hesitant to enter Casa Lau for the first time because they had never met me before, but Teti was at a total loss, and they felt he needed their support."

Mami starts to cry, so I get up in search for a tissue. "No need," Mami says as she pulls out a napkin. "I fold one of the sleeves of my dress like this and tuck in a napkin. I keep one there because I get teary eyes all the time. It's handy."

I sit back down and Mami continues.

"When I saw Tío Neto and Tío Carlos walking in, I was so touched by their caring support for our family which had never opened our doors to them that I embraced them both silently. And since that time and without a word, Tío Neto and Tío Carlos openly became part of the Lau family and were welcomed as Teti's sons and in a lot of ways as my sons, too. You were barely a few months old when all this happened. So you have never known anything differently. Tío Neto and Tío Carlos have always been there as your uncles, which is the way it should be."

Mami seems calmer than before. So I ask her if she wants to continue putting things away. She is hungry and gets up to grab a snack. She brews some coffee and gets the bag of sweet breads. While I watch her sip a hot cup of coffee and eat a piece of sweet bread, my mouth is salivating and I grab a *concha* and split it in half. Then, Mami finishes the other half of the *concha* while I reach for a *sope*. Mami just smiles since she knows that *sopes* and *conchas* are my favourite sweet breads. Then, she continues telling me about Casa Lau after Tío Pepe's death.

"With the return of your aunts and uncles to Casa Lau

and as the family grew larger, Papito decided it was time
for the house to keep up with the pace. A couple of years
after you were born, our house on top of the store and the
warehouses were built. With this addition, our living space
was moved from being behind to being above the store. Then
one more level was built, which serves as our *azotea*, as well
as a small room and bathroom for a maid. This room was
rarely used after being built since, by then, you three girls
were in charge of the cleaning and house chores."

Tío Carlos (centre) and Tío Neto (right)
listening to Tío Carlos (Tía Lupe's husband) at
Teti's 80th birthday party in Hotel Kamico (1980).

Casa Lau (1988).

Casa Lau became a large structure; from the front, the building is two stories, and from the back at the bottom of the hill, it is four stories high. The building is rather wide, but it is even deeper from front to back, occupying almost one city block. The addition of an entire floor to be used as living space allowed the warehouse to be expanded when Casa Lau was growing. In spite of having three levels of warehouse space, Casa Lau needed more. The wall between the *cantina* and the store was knocked down to give more space and to enlarge the store. For additional warehouse space, the building next to us was leased and a door on the wall in between was created for access. Also for warehouse space, a large building across the street from Casa Lau was rented.

Shortly after moving everyone to our new home, things began shifting once again. Papito and Mamita had Vero, so now Mami could busy herself babysitting her three granddaughters. Mincho was no longer with us, so after watching him closely for so many years, Mami was happy to take full responsibility for the kitchen. Tía Chony decided to leave for Mexico City for a secretarial course and soon after secured a job. Tía Lupe and Tío Juanca stayed a few more years and after finishing high school left Casa Lau to join Tía Chony in Mexico City to go to university; Tía Lupe went to UNAM and Tío Juanca to La Salle.

Mami felt as if she was once again losing her children.

"At the time I did not understand why everyone had to leave again. I understand now that's the way of life. But because I had no say and the kids never talked to me about their schooling since I would not have understood, I felt that all the decisions were made without my input. The only good thing is that since we all lived together, I could focus on looking after you three girls."

Tía Chony, Tía Lupe, and Tío Juanca lived in a centrally-located four-storey building on *Artículo 123* and *Ayuntamiento* in Mexico City. It was a spacious two-bedroom apartment with long living and dining room areas, a small kitchen, and a bathroom between the two bedrooms. It was on the top floor and had hardwood flooring throughout except in the kitchen and the bathroom, which were tiled. There were no heaters and a sweater was a must even in summer. On the roof, there were small bedrooms for the maids and also clotheslines in individual fenced-in "cages" for each apartment in the building. The lobby, hallway, and staircases always seemed dark and cold. The old-style elevator looked grand with its polished brass, a see-through metal sliding door, and a very well-mannered porter. The larger bedroom was big enough for three single beds, a couple of dressers and bedside tables, and a bureau with mirror for Tía Chony, Tía Lupe, and a close friend named Cande to share. Tío Juanca stayed in the smaller bedroom, which was spacious enough to hold two single beds and a table that functioned as a working desk.

"I tried to be as good as a mother could be from far away. I made sure the apartment was well-furnished and had everything the children needed. Every time I heard that a friend or relative was flying to Mexico City, I would go downstairs to Casa Lau and reach up the shelves to get cans, dried goods, soaps, and toilet paper and pack them in boxes together with frozen meats and Chinese buns that I had made to be sent. Even though they were expensive, Tía Chony, Tía Lupe, and Tío Juanca would get plane tickets to come home every time they wanted and could, especially for Christmas."

"To allow them to concentrate on their studies, I even got a young woman in Tapachula to stay in Mexico City to do the cleaning and cooking in the apartment. I had hired Lluvia originally to do house chores in Casa Lau. But I noticed that she could cook, learned quickly, and was able to work without much supervision. She was young and gladly accepted the offer of going to such a big and exciting place to take care of the cleaning and cooking in return for a salary, food, and lodging, Sundays off, and being in Mexico City. Do you remember her with her long, black hair? Lluvia eventually got married and stayed to start a family."

Mami gets up and rinses her cup and my glass. I close and put away the bag of sweet breads so that no ants get to it. For some reason, ants quickly appear and surround anything sweet left in the open. So I also wipe the table twice making sure there are no traces of sugary crumbs.

"I think I'm going to bed." Mami says. "We can leave the cleaning of Casa Lau for tomorrow." I remind her that we are going to the beach tomorrow. Then she responds, "Let's do it the day after tomorrow then."

16

GENERATIONS

THIS morning Tía Elda and Tío Carlos pick us up to go to the beach about thirty kilometres away. They both know that the beach is a special place where I spent a lot of my childhood swimming, building different things with sand, riding the surf on an air mattress, playing volleyball, watching sunsets, and spending time with family and friends. When I was in my teens, Papito together with his brothers and sisters owned a piece of waterfront land where we spent every Sunday, Christmas, New Year's, and long weekend. Although the land was recently sold to another *paisano*, Tío Carlos asks for permission to use the palm leaf *palapa*, the pool, and the indoor bathroom. Mami does not like the beach since she cannot swim and thinks it is too hot, but this time she comes along as Doña Lolita, Tía Elda's mother, also wants to go. So Mami will have somebody her age she knows well to talk with while we "youngsters" play in the water.

Playa Linda looks very different. The bumpy and dusty gravel road we used to drive on is now paved. There are also many more houses and more sophisticated-looking ones than the rustic retreats or bare lots with only *palapas* I was accustomed to seeing. Tío Carlos explains to me that more people reside here than when it was used solely as a weekend getaway. The waves are also larger than I remember and, though many years back it was known to be a deserted beach, I now see many more people strolling and fishing. This area used to be called *la tiburonera* (a place that has sharks) because it is open to the sea, where sharks were caught. In addition, there was a processing plant located somewhere on this stretch of beach where sharks would be cut open, cleaned, and packaged for export.

Though I feel a bit of disappointment because of all the changes, at the same time I try to convince myself that they are for the better, though better for whom or than what I am not sure. At the very least, I am glad to know that the familiar scent of salt and the magnificent sound of the crashing waves still have a magic way with me even now when I close my eyes in front of this beach.

After I go swimming with Tío Carlos, we join Mami, Tía Elda, and Doña Lolita under the *palapa*. We get some drinking water and sit down to enjoy some *tamales* stuffed with chicken in *mole* sauce wrapped in a banana leaf. Since this is the last chance I will have to eat any in a long time, Tía Elda gives me two larger ones. For some reason, food tastes especially delicious at the beach after a nice swim. Then, while we eat the usual beach snack of tuna salad on crackers, we reminisce about one particular time we ended up staying the night in this spot in hammocks with only one of our uncles volunteering to supervise all of us nine kids, while the other adults returned to their beds in Tapachula to avoid the bugs and the mosquitoes. We sure had good times in this place.

We pick everything up after we finish eating and laughing about all those funny moments we have spent on this lot. Then I take Mami for a short stroll so that she can get some exercise, while Tía Elda stays to chat with her mom and Tío Carlos takes his customary afternoon *siesta*. Mami is very relaxed and continues telling me what happened after my aunts and uncle left to Mexico City for their studies. Mami says that the following years became the best ones of her life. Everything was peaceful and ordinary and her only preoccupations were mostly to do with cooking and looking after her granddaughters.

"For some reason both your sisters always cried at night. Just so your Mom would get some sleep, I would place Guada when she was a baby [and years later Vero] on the hammock in our bedroom [on the other side of the house] and rock her until she closed her eyes. Besides, I didn't need to go down to the store and your Mom did."

"You girls misbehaved all the time. When your parents punished or scolded you, Teti and I came to your rescue every time, kept you hidden in the kitchen or in our room away from an upset Mamita trying to reach you with a metal ruler or a leather belt. You should be thankful we intervened most of the time."

"I spoiled you, too," Mami admits. "I tried to make as often as I could the foods you liked. And I kept those dishes aside so when you came home from school at 1:00 p.m., I could give you a treat. It was nice to see you girls eat those treats as if you would never eat them again. And it made it all worthwhile just to hear you say, *'Hou hou sek, Ah-Mami'* ('Very, very yummy, Mami')."

Mami's greatest accomplishment was in the kitchen. She enjoyed spending time in her *oficina* preparing day-to-day meals or creating complicated and time-consuming delicacies. Most of her cooking was obviously Chinese since that is what she knew and what Teti liked. She was constantly thinking about what she was going to cook for lunch while she was still eating breakfast. As soon as she sat down and took up her chopsticks, she would unfailingly ask what we wanted for the next meal or what we thought about having steamed chicken with green onions and ginger that night. And most important for her was what kind of soup she would cook every day since Teti always wanted to have soup even in the mornings. Mami was also careful about cooking with very little salt because of Teti's health, and she got her greatest satisfaction when people gave her a much-deserved compliment for her cooking.

Thanks to Mami and Mamita, I was able to prepare some dishes for myself and avoid starvation when I moved away from home. Having to cook at least three full meals a day and for so many people, Mami always needed any help she could get in the kitchen. Around 4:00 p.m., before we went to English lessons or on Saturday afternoons when Casa Lau was not very busy, Mami would ask us to wash and cut vegetables or sort grains of rice and beans, while she focused on some other task in preparation for that evening's or the next day's cooking. Even when things were busy and hectic in the kitchen, Mami would take the time to explain how and why she did what she did and how to check for smells and pay attention to freshness: fish with clear eyeballs, vibrant red colour in raw beef, firm raw shrimp, no sour smells from milk products. I think teaching her cooking skills and inspiration in the kitchen was definitely another of Mami's accomplishments.

"After Tía Chony, Tía Lupe, and Tío Juanca finished their studies in Mexico City," Mami says, "Teti and I felt that our work as parents was done and we told them that we didn't care what they studied, that we only wanted them to graduate from university, technical school, or college. After that, they all could go anywhere and do anything they wanted. This was the only thing we expected in return from them." For both Mami and Teti, the education of their children was the most important and valuable thing they could provide them with.

After Tía Lupe got married and then Tía Chony, Mami busied herself with taking care of the next set of grandchildren. "I enjoyed taking care of Tía Lupe and Tía Chony's kids. I was hopeful I could spend more time with my grandchildren than I had with my own children. So I asked your aunts to drop off their kids early in the morning and most afternoons so I could look after them. I also spent endless hours making baby and kids' foods with the freshest ingredients. You were already grown up and begged me to give you some of the children's rice porridge, which I steamed with that day's chopped up boneless *robalo* filets for at least two hours. The porridge was very tasty because I only used fresh fish. I didn't believe in Gerber (and still don't), so I steamed vegetables and mashed all kinds of fruit for my grandkids every day. And I never allowed them to have any leftovers because these aren't nutritious at all for children. So I ate any leftovers instead of giving it to the kids."

It is too hot to be out in the sun. Mami and I return to where the *palapa* is, looking for some shade. I notice that Mami needs to sit down and drink some water after our stroll on the beach. Tío Carlos wakes up from his siesta, and Tía Elda asks if we are ready to head back into town.

On our way home, we stop by to buy a couple of cold, fresh coconuts. Since Mami and I have not been in this area in a while, Tío Carlos gives us a tour driving by the new port where cruise ships now make a scheduled stop every once in a while. I am surprised to see this new structure and cannot help but wonder if the resources to build such a port on this spot could have been used more wisely somewhere else.

17

RADICAL
CHANGES

MAMI and I are getting ready for our departure tomorrow morning. I have packed a small suitcase with all my clothes and am also bringing back to Vancouver from Casa Lau a few items that have special meaning. Mami has washed all her clothing that she keeps in Casa Lau and is folding and putting it away in her closet. She is not taking anything with her back to Campeche. She places on her bed the same set of clothes she initially brought with her from Campeche to change into before our flight.

Since Mami would not have it any other way, we have divided the rest of the tasks between the two of us. To avoid any arguments, I have decided just to follow instructions from Mami though I know she will end up doing more than she should. Mami cleans her bedroom, her bathroom, and the kitchen, while I am in charge of the living room, all the corridors, and the rest of the areas we used while we were here. Then I empty and clean the refrigerator and the stove, and put back all the dishes, pots, and pans where they were and cover them with a cotton cloth so they do not get too dusty and dirty while the house sits empty.

While I am putting things away in the kitchen, Mami comes in and continues where she had left off yesterday at the beach.

"I was busy taking care of Tía Lupe and Tía Chony's children. By this time, Teti was well into his seventies and became very ill. Teti had arthritis, gout, and kidney problems. He also couldn't walk well because of a bone that was rubbing his lower spine. So he had surgery in Houston to remove part of this bone. After surgery, he depended on a cane and, if you remember, also a walker. During that time, it seemed like we were going from one doctor to another. We saw doctors in Tapachula and even in Mexico City and Houston. I felt bad for Teti because he got treatment after treatment and then ended up in hospital."

So every day, Mami would divide her time between the hospital and home and prepare all his meals. That left Mamita to assume kitchen responsibilities for the household. Once Teti left the *Seguro Social* (the government-run hospital), he did not want to return. There was no way he would have gone to the hospital of his own will. He was a stubborn person who even if he could not walk, somehow ended up carrying boxes and serving customers in the store. But that was something no one wanted him to do when he went back home.

Teti spent his last few years bedridden in Casa Lau. He

had to be taken care of twenty-four hours a day and insisted on staying in Tío Juanca's old room so that Mami could get some rest in their bedroom. He kept his cool and his sense of humour in spite of having his active and social life reduced to one room and limited daily visits from his grown children and friends. After school, we would come directly to see him and sit beside him just to chat and joke around. He would take advantage of his limited movement and would request, as he always had, his daily massage. With our fists, we would start pounding his legs, arms, and shoulders; when he would not ask us to stop and we felt too much time had gone by, the pounding speed and strength would increase until Teti would give up and wave us to go do our homework.

One morning in January 1984, Teti passed away. His body lay in an open casket in *Funerales Bravo* for a couple of days, where thousands of people came to pay their respects. On the morning of the funeral, Mami and I sat in the front seat of the hearse, holding hands and crying the entire way. Behind us, a long procession of family, friends, *paisanos*, members of the business community, customers, and everyone who had known him followed the hearse on foot to the *panteón* where he was buried. That was the first and only time I saw Casa Lau closed down and a black bow hanging on the front door as a sign of mourning. It was the day I truly grasped the immense hole Teti was leaving in people's lives.

Months later, when I left for the United States to study

and experienced firsthand the loneliness of being by myself in a different country, I had the strange feeling that Teti was beside me keeping me company. A year later when I returned home for a visit, I felt emptiness in Casa Lau without Teti's songs and jokes and smiles. It was then my turn to truly understand how important he had been in my life and how fortunate I had been to grow up with him.

It is late and Tío Carlos and Tía Elda will pick us up for our last dinner in Tapachula. They have chosen an outdoor family place that serves a local dish called *garnachas*, which are two-inch round corn *tortillas* deep fried in pork fat and covered with a beef and tomato sauce and crumbled cheese. Mami wants to stay home as she feels the need to tidy up. So I promise to return in an hour and ask her if she wants me to bring her a *cena de pollo*, chicken cooked in tomato sauce, Teti's favourite dish.

When we were kids, we used to take a pot and pick up a couple of orders from Doña Chole, the most famous source of this kind of local dish. We also brought along a separate container for *garnachas*, since they were another of her specialties. Tonight, Tío Carlos wants me to try some of these deep-fried *tortillas* to compare them with the ones Doña Chole used to make. Mami does not want chicken and instead wants me to bring her six *garnachas* since she has not had any in a long time either. She says that *garnachas* do not exist in Campeche (they have *panuchos* instead), which she likes as well but which are totally different in taste (*garnachas* are made of beef in a tomato and chili sauce while *panuchos* are made of chicken marinated in *achiote*), in size (*garnachas* are much smaller than *panuchos*), and in texture (*garnachas* are less crunchy than *panuchos*).

I remember how things began shifting once again in Casa Lau after Teti's death. My parents' dream had always been to provide us with a good education that would lead to a wider range of choices for us as adults. In their eyes, sending their children abroad to study was the only way they thought we would learn independence, self-reliance, different perspectives and ways of doing. After finishing high school, and in late August 1984, Guada left to go to Victoria, in British Columbia, to attend twelfth grade in a boarding school in preparation for university studies. Since Mamita's closest sibling (her older brother, #6) lived in nearby Vancouver, Victoria seemed to be the perfect city to send my sister to; Victoria was far enough for Guada to learn to be on her own, but at the same time it was close enough to Vancouver and uncle #6 for any emergencies that may have come up. A year later, in 1985, I left for Delaware, in the United States, to finish high school. Mamita's niece May, daughter of my mother's older brother, #4, was doing her Ph.D. there and offered to give me a room to stay. Then, in 1987, Vero was sent to study in Quebec, where my sister Guada had moved from Victoria to go to university.

Mami tells me that, suddenly, Casa Lau was simply not the same. At first, it felt empty without Teti and without her live-in granddaughters. When we had left for our studies, Mami experienced the same ache she had felt as when she had said good-bye to her own children in Hong Kong many years back. Fortunately, she soon noticed that Mamita and Papito needed her to be around the house to help out with small chores and even for her opinion on certain matters related to the store. She also filled the void by seeing more of and focusing on her younger grandchildren, my aunts' Tía Lupe and Tía Chony's children. At the same time, Mami rediscovered how much she enjoyed her kitchen duties and realized that she had time to reunite with her social circle of *paisana* friends to play *mah-jong*. But that routine only lasted a few years.

"Your mother was thin and tired and got sick more and more frequently," Mami says to me. "Everyone thought it was because she missed you, her three daughters. When you were small, your mother looked after you with one eye and ran the store with the other. Every afternoon you headed down the staircase to the store so that your mother, without abandoning her store duties, could help you with your homework or patiently teach you to read and write Chinese characters or force you to type what seemed to be hundreds of exercise sheets on Papito's gigantic typewriter. After dinner your mother continued her role of mother by giving you piano lessons; she watched you painfully practising this instrument that gave her pleasure and refuge, and she is still so good at playing. And before going to bed she spent long nights sewing your school uniforms, all of your clothing, and dance costumes that your school required you to wear during performances. Mamita even made your white Communion gown, a two-layered long dress made with taffeta and fine lace. Your mother has always been a great seamstress, unlike me."

Even with a full schedule, Mamita was in charge of making certain dishes. One was steamed duck in star anise sauce, which she taught me how to make. So, when Teti was hospitalized and it became time for her to be responsible for cooking, she did it well and without any problems. It was then that I had to learn how to cook entire dishes. After school, I would call the store from the kitchen and Mamita would give me exact instructions on how to make that day's lunch. With one hand on the phone while serving customers at the store and supervising employees, Mamita would listen to me describe what I was attempting to cook in the kitchen on the other end of the line, just above her on the second floor. This way, food would be ready by the time Casa Lau closed down at 2:00 p.m. and we could all eat together.

During the little spare time Mamita had, she baked. She would make butter cookies, cakes, and fruit pies, my favourite being the one she made with a filling of whole cream and bananas. She splurged on baking books and a quality mixer as well as cake pans and cookie cutters. Even though she must have felt tired, she had the patience to teach us three young girls. She would let us read recipes, mix ingredients, play with the dough, be inventive with our cookie shapes, and encourage us to bake.

But after working long hours for more than twenty years in Casa Lau without at least one full day of rest, Mamita's health was failing. She'd had to manage with the stress of being in the store dealing with the public and with employees day-in and day-out. She never had time to exercise and rarely had a good night of sleep because of the constant noise coming through the open windows of her bedroom. It was time for Mamita to take a break and concentrate on her health. After much thought and discussion and with certain apprehension, it was decided Casa Lau would have to close down.

"It was a tough and painful decision because Casa Lau represented Teti's life and legacy and was a big part of the Lau family. But in the end, I accepted it with much resignation as a decision that had to be made. Though, at the time," Mami turns and looks at me and says, "I was hopeful that YOU would take over the store since I noticed that you spent more time than anybody else in Casa Lau other than your parents and Teti." I nod in agreement and feel she is right on the dot in expressing this. The truth was that I loved being and working in the store and had dreamed of returning to run Casa Lau some day.

With Guada and Vero already studying in Quebec, Mamita and Papito applied for the entire family to immigrate to Canada. For Mamita's health, Mamita and Papito decided to try settling in Vancouver, where Mamita's brother #6 was a doctor and could guide them in finding suitable medical assistance. Mamita was suffering from allergies, sudden heart palpitations, high blood pressure, poor blood circulation, and insomnia to name a few conditions. Later, once we found living accommodations, Mami would join us in Vancouver. After all the necessary paperwork, interviews, and doctor examinations, Mamita and Papito received our landed immigrant visas, which coincided with Vero's graduation from a CEGEP (College of General and Vocational Education) in Quebec and my graduation from an American university (the University of Nevada, Las Vegas). The plan was for Mamita, Papito, Vero, and me to go by car through the western United States and "land" in the province of British Columbia in August 1990. Guada, finishing her studies in Quebec and unable to take the trip, drove to the Canada-U.S. border nearest to her on the east coast and re-entered Canada officially as a landed immigrant by herself shortly thereafter.

After Mamita and Papito left for Vancouver, Mami stayed on in Casa Lau. As stubborn as she has always been, she refused to live with any of my aunts or neighbours. She said she had never gone against Papito's wishes, but she simply wanted to be home. Under the condition that a live-in maid would stay with her and that she would regularly call Tía Lupe, who then lived about ten minutes away by car, Mami remained in Casa Lau for a couple of years. She would also cross the street to check in with Tía Nelly in *Kam Long* restaurant every afternoon and agreed to have Papito fly from Vancouver every six months to visit her during those two years.

After a couple of years of having maids coming and going, stealing from her, and simply refusing to do the only chore of cleaning the part of the house in use, Mami confessed to Papito that her living arrangements were not working out. The only choice was to move in with Tía Lupe, who was her only child living in Tapachula. By then, Tía Chony was living in Guatemala, Tío Juanca was in San Francisco, and Papito was in Vancouver. Not wanting to be a burden, Mami moved in with Tía Lupe with the condition that she would be in charge of cooking the family meals. In addition to cooking duties, Mami enjoyed having once again grandchildren around the house, this time Tía Lupe's three daughters.

After a few years went by, Tía Lupe's husband (another Tío Carlos) got a job offer in Campeche, approximately 900 kilometres northeast of Tapachula in the state of Campeche on the Gulf of Mexico. Tía Lupe's daughters were getting ready to go to university and would not be heading to Campeche. So, once again, Mami found herself toying with the idea of moving back to Casa Lau since she missed her home. But this time she thought to herself that if she moved back, she would never leave her house.

However, Papito discussed with her only two viable options. Mami had to choose between Campeche or finally moving to Vancouver, where Papito had already looked into sponsoring her. My sisters and I were thrilled with the idea of Mami moving to Vancouver. To get her excited, we would call her to discuss where she would like to live, how she could play *mah-jong*, and eat *dim sum* every day if she wanted to, the proximity of a Chinatown to where she would be and above all the frequency we would be able to see her. But in the end, Mami decided to try Campeche.

"It's too cold in Canada for me. I'd have to wear too many layers all the time, and it would be too uncomfortable. Your father would have to buy me travel insurance, which is expensive. I think that if I got sick, the treatments and medicines would be expensive, too. I wouldn't want to be a burden and I think the health system over there would not suit an old woman like me."

"It was a difficult decision not to choose going to Vancouver to live with Papito because he is my eldest son. But then I thought it was time for Papito to let go of the never-ending responsibility of taking care of me. After all, this was Mexico and not China, and we were now living in different times. So I followed Tía Lupe to live in Campeche and left Casa Lau, my adopted hometown of Tapachula, and my small circle of friends. Though many years had passed since their deaths and as silly as it may sound, I felt I was also abandoning Teti and Tío Pepe. It was a very uneasy feeling for me."

18

REFLECTIONS

IT is 4:30 a.m. when Mami wakes me up. It is a bit chilly, but I am just focusing on getting ready and taking our luggage down to the *portón*. Mami inspects the entire house and covers the furniture and the beds with some sheets, while I check that the gas lines for the stove and the water heater are completely shut off. Then, I make sure every window is closed and every door is locked. I also go around closing all the custom-made drapes, which are already stained from the strong sun and are a bit torn from close to thirty years of use.

There is no time for breakfast, but Mami insists on carrying a few cookies in a napkin in case we get hungry. So with her arm in one of my hands, we slowly descend the yellow staircase. I leave Mami waiting where we used to store the sacks of sugar. Then I leap two steps at a time and climb back up to make a final inspection. I run around every room again with an ache in my heart, and finally lock the wooden door and head downstairs to join Mami.

"Are you going to see your parents as soon as you arrive back in Vancouver?" Mami asks while we are waiting.

"Most likely I'll visit them as soon as I get there, and don't worry, I won't forget to give my mother the bag of freshly-made *mole* you bought for her."

"You look more like your mother than your sisters do. They look more like your father, Papito. Did you know that your mother was the most beautiful young woman I had ever seen when I first met her?"

Unlike Mami's, Mamita's marriage to Papito had not been arranged.

"Many young Mexican women in Tapachula," Mami continues, "befriended your father with the hopes of a future marriage. He was a handsome, charming, and well-educated young Chinese man. And even those *macho* Mexican fathers did not mind their daughters going after your father because they were under the impression that Casa Lau would eventually belong to him. He was considered a good catch. But when your father saw your mother in a photo while he was studying in Hong Kong, I think that was it for him."

"Papito asked his friend, who had shown him Mamita's picture, to see your mother in person, and they finally met in a café in Macau. They dated for a short time and decided to get married. Teti and I flew to Hong Kong and first met Mamita on a cold fall day when we asked Mamita's mother, your Grandma Ah-Popo, for Mamita's hand in marriage. I was speechless when I met your mother since she was a beautiful, shy, and intelligent nineteen-year-old woman who had been raised in Macau and educated in Hong Kong. Being a cold day, your mother, Mamita, was wearing thick clothes, which made her look larger than she really was. Being a bit 'round' and therefore healthy meant that we could expect healthy grandchildren soon. It was like a dream come true. Teti wanted Papito to marry a Chinese girl, and I had wished for a healthy daughter-in-law."

Mami also learned bits and pieces about Mamita's family background during that trip. The family had endured difficult times and seemed resilient and strong, which both Mami and Teti thought to be very important traits. Her family had left southern China, escaping from the Communist regime, and settled in Macau, then a Portuguese enclave. Mamita's father, my Grandpa Ah-Kung, was a self-made, successful entrepreneur who owned a few jewelry stores in southern China and Malaysia. This success allowed him and Grandma Ah-Popo to have seven children. Mamita is the sixth child and the youngest girl in a family of five boys and two girls. Unfortunately, Mamita's father died very young from a stroke after news arrived that the Communists were seizing his Chinese stores. Mamita was about three years old. Being Ah-Kung's favourite child of all seven, Mamita felt short-changed. Even now, she angrily talks about how the Communists robbed her of the opportunity to enjoy her father's presence and life.

Ah-Popo, now a widow with a strong character and an

extremely active and nurturing woman, was left to raise the family. The ages between Mamita's older and younger siblings was wide enough so that when Ah-Kung died, Mamita's eldest brothers, #1 and #2, were already in charge of the jewelry stores in Malaysia. With much perseverance through tough times, Ah-Popo and her two eldest sons provided for everyone in the family. By the time Mamita and Papito got engaged, Mamita's family had reached a certain prosperity and stability.

It was not until my parents' wedding day that Mami noticed my mother was actually extremely thin and small – her waist hardly measured 20 inches. I could barely fit into her wedding *cheung sam* (Chinese long dress) when I was thirteen and wore it for Tapachula's yearly parade.

"Immediately after I saw this," Mami says, "I stopped at a Chinese medicine pharmacy and asked for all these herbs. From then on, I made every single medicinal soup available to get your mother a little fat and healthy to have babies. Your mother was very obedient and followed all my instructions after I returned to Tapachula while they stayed in Hong Kong. Your mother eventually became pregnant almost three years later."

Mami tells me that in a lot of ways, Mamita reminded her of herself. Mamita was young, inexperienced in the kitchen, lived faraway from her own family in a place she had not chosen, and had to struggle with a new language

Mamita (third from the left) and Mami (on the right) at a family gathering a few days after Mamita's wedding in Kowloon (1963).

that seemed difficult to master. When Mamita arrived in Tapachula pregnant with Guada, Mami saw her own life reflected in her daughter-in-law and resolved to be a good mother-in-law. Besides, Mami was extremely happy and proud since she had the most beautiful daughter-in-law who was carrying the Lau family's first grandchild.

Throughout those twenty-five years that Mami and Mamita lived under the same roof, their relationship was marked by mutual respect. Mami looked after the kitchen and the household, while Mamita was a mother and worked long hours in Casa Lau. There was a natural fit between the different roles they assumed, and neither one trampled on the other's responsibilities, duties, and space. The only time Mami and Teti "interfered" was when it came down to us, their granddaughters, and only to spoil us as any grandparent would.

On my birthday, I usually received a red envelope and Mamita would make an orange or chocolate cake. It was a small family event and nothing else. So when I turned seven, I wanted to have a birthday party with a big cake, two or three *piñatas*, candies, music, games, and presents the way most Mexican kids at school celebrated their birthday every year. My parents opposed to the idea because they believed that children should learn that a party or gift was a meaningful gesture, a reward for somebody's accomplishments, and a special occasion to celebrate a rite of passage. Seeing how disappointed I was, Mami told my parents that she would take care of everything for my birthday party and Teti told them that I deserved to have such a party because I had good grades at school. With Mami and Teti vouching for me, Mamita and Papito gave in, and I had the seventh birthday party I had dreamed of having.

Both Mami and Mamita asked each other's opinions in various subjects like family, the store, and meals, and there were never any loud quarrels. Mami tells me that, even when there were disagreements, Mamita never raised her voice against Mami and most often Mamita would accept defeat and keep her grumbling to herself. Mamita played the perfect role as daughter-in-law. Mami says that she always acknowledged Mamita's place in the family as significant and important, being the wife of her eldest son. And she admits that Mamita's respect and silent acceptance of Mami and Teti's place in the family hierarchy followed a sense of Chinese tradition that kept us living together in relative peace and harmony for many years.

Mami thinks that, just like herself, there was perhaps a feeling of loneliness in Mamita. Living in Tapachula and working all the time was not easy. Mamita only had a handful of friends, mostly Chinese women (*paisanas*). In a full house such as Casa Lau, she had rarely time for herself or any privacy. She also managed to return to Macau, where her own mother was living, only a few times. Perhaps one of the most enjoyable times for Mamita was when Ah-Popo came and stayed with us for approximately eight months. She was the only person from Mamita's side of the family who visited while she lived in Tapachula. I know that for Mamita, having her own mother there for these eight months was something special and memorable.

Mamita's alienation because of living far from family and friends resonated with me after I left home. Looking back at her life, I noticed as if her being was not entirely in Tapachula. How else could she feel? Mamita spent most of her married life surrounded by strangers and living with Papito's family. Family reunions from her side of the family were hard to come by. Mamita's family was and still is scattered around the world: Malaysia, Macau, Hong Kong, England, Australia, the United States, and Canada to name only a few places.

While growing up, I met only a few of Mamita's side of the family. My first trip to Hong Kong and Macau was when I was three years old. During this trip, I met Ah-Popo, and Mamita's brothers #4 and #7, as well as her older and only sister. Truthfully I can only remember receiving lots of presents from everyone we met and everywhere we went and not much about Mamita's family.

Mamita's brother #6, with whom she has always seemed to be closest, lives in Vancouver. I met him for the first time when I was five during a visit Mamita, my sister Guada, and I made to him in England when he was finishing medical school. Though I have never met Mamita's brothers #1 and #2, and have never had contact with most of my cousins, Mamita told us stories and showed us pictures whenever she received letters or packages from far away. In spite of trying to maintain a strong emotional connection, the absence of physical contact with her family must have been difficult to endure for Mamita.

At 5:30 a.m. sharp, Tío Carlos and Tía Elda are outside honking and ringing the doorbell. We get the luggage inside their Pontiac and head to the airport. We arrive on time to check in for our 7:00 a.m. flight and without any complications go through Customs and Immigration checkpoints.

Upon hearing the announcement of our flight, we get up from sitting on hard plastic chairs in the departures area. Mami holds her cane and makes sure her purse hangs comfortably from her shoulder. She turns around to say good-bye. With tears in our eyes, we hug and kiss both Tío Carlos and Tía Elda. Then, we slowly walk towards the tarmac and the plane, once in a while turning back to wave to Tío and Tía. I can feel that Mami is as upset as I am.

In these last two weeks, I have been given a second chance to relive some of my childhood memories by listening to Mami, by being in Casa Lau, by smelling those familiar scents and hearing those sounds, by watching her cook again. I have discovered that I feel as comfortable being with Mami in Casa Lau as if there had been no interruptions in the last seventeen years. After all this, I do not want to leave the comfort, the familiarity, the sense of belonging, and the feeling of coming full circle. Most importantly, in this short time, I have come to realize that my relationship with Mami is an unbreakable bond: between grandmother and granddaughter, between two women who are strongly connected and will remain so no matter how far apart we are, how frequently we see one another, or how different our times and our experiences we each have lived and will face. Yes. An unexplainable yet remarkable connection.

The flight to Mexico City is brief and quiet. We manage to get some scrambled eggs and orange juice for breakfast on the plane. Mami seems to have a lot on her mind and only turns around once and says, "It really was a good idea to spend time together in Casa Lau."

"I am glad you accepted my invitation to come with me." I nod in agreement and with a knot in my throat I am barely able to blurt out, "If you hadn't come, it would have been quite boring all by myself and without anybody to make me eat all the time."

She just smiles and returns to her thoughts.

I, too, immerse myself in my own thoughts. After getting to know a bit more about Mami's and Teti's lives, and for that matter Papito's and Mamita's as well as my own, I realize how many more questions now linger in my mind than when

I started two weeks ago asking Mami questions.

Did Teti accomplish what he had set out to do when he left Kau Kong in China at eighteen years of age? How did he endure those years during the Japanese Invasion of not knowing if his wife and son were alive? Was he happy with the way his children had grown up in Mexico in spite of the fact that his goal of returning with his family to Hong Kong and China never materialized? Did Teti think his children had become "Chinese" enough? Were Tapachula and Mexico the place he would eventually call home?

My mind wanders off to Papito and his life. What does he remember of the first ten years of his life when he was fatherless and running away from the Japanese? How did he feel about meeting his father in Tapachula, a strange land faraway from his birthplace in China? What does he think about giving up the job offer and a life in Hong Kong, and instead choosing to take over Casa Lau and return to Tapachula? Does he feel that moving to Vancouver instead of staying in Tapachula was the right choice? I conclude that I will need to approach Papito and ask him.

Then, my mind shifts towards the groups of Chinese men who left China for a better life and headed to various parts of the world. Did they feel they had accomplished their goals in another land? Did their decision to leave China give them the better life they were looking for? How did they manage during those years of separation, uncertainty, and loneliness they endured away from their families and their home countries? Were they able to provide for their families the way they had envisioned? How are their stories different and similar to each other's? How is each Chinese man's story different and similar to Teti's? And what about the groups of Chinese men who, like my father, chose to immigrate a third time and reside not in China, not in Mexico, but in Canada? I realize the questions are daunting and the answers are unknowable.

After we arrive, Mami will take a plane to Campeche, and I will head to Vancouver. Luckily, my cousin Jenny is meeting up with Mami at the *Aeropuerto Internacional de México* to keep her company and to help her get safely onto the next flight to her final destination. Her blood pressure cannot handle the altitude, so Mami cannot spend too many hours in Mexico City without feeling sick.

As with my earlier flight to Tapachula, I do not have much time to make my connecting flight to Vancouver; I have to hurry to the other side of the terminal to international departures to check in. Fortunately, I do not have to worry about anything else since my luggage has been tagged to meet me at my final destination; I just have to run fast enough to the Continental Airlines counter, go through Immigration to exit Mexico, and finally get to my gate before the plane leaves.

Mami and I wait at the arrival gate for a wheelchair. I do

not want to leave her so quickly, but I know she will be taken to the appropriate arrival area where my cousin is waiting for her. Once the wheelchair arrives, I hug her and kiss her right cheek and we both start crying. She hugs me back very tightly and cannot let go easily. With all the noise around us, I can barely hear Mami whispering in my ear.

"Ah-Mey, this is the last time we will see each other, so I want you to know that Mami feels privileged you came from so far away just to see an old lady. You take care of your father and your mother; listen to your husband and don't go without him for too long; don't work too much and take care of your health; and start having kids because pretty soon you'll be too old to have them."

I know that it is more important that I give her a big smile and that we make this short and sweet for both our sakes.

"Mami, I promise I'll call you tonight when I get to Vancouver." I assure her in a loud voice. "We'll see each other in a few months when I come back for my business trip; so this is NOT the last time we will see each other."

Before I start running, Mami sits down on the wheelchair, turns around and has enough time to say, *"Nei siu sam nei chi kei"* ("Pay attention to yourself") in Chinese, followed by the same words but in Spanish, *"Cuídate mucho."*

I hear her and answer back, "Mami – you, too, take care of yourself."

EPILOGUE

THOSE two weeks in November 2002 would be the last time Mami and/or I stayed in Casa Lau for an extended period. It was even perhaps the last time Casa Lau witnessed and felt the presence of anybody in the family within its walls: the sounds and the smells of everyday living, the hope of birth and the pain of death, the laughter, the tears, the screaming, the secrets, and the madness of three generations living under one roof.

It was during this trip to Tapachula that Mami brought up the idea of writing a book about her life. She watched me quietly and very intently for the first few days as I prepared my taperecorder and made frantic notes to interview some *paisanos* for my master's thesis. Then, one afternoon as we were sitting down to eat lunch, Mami said, "Ah-Mey, now that I am old, I have a lot of things to say. You and I should write a book; I will answer anything you want to know, and I will talk about everything I can remember; though you will have to think of the questions to ask and write the entire book yourself."

Following her words and my desire to know more about Mami and about myself, I began a series of conversations that would give me enough material to write this piece. These conversations, planned and unplanned, took place sitting on her bed in her room, in the dining room when we were dipping our sweet breads into a cup of coffee, in her *oficina* while she was preparing something special for lunch or to give away, and in the living room in between her *telenovelas*, initially in Tapachula and continuing in Campeche from 2002 through 2006. Some of these conversations even took place via phone when, because of the distance, I felt I needed to hear her response to something that just could not wait until my next visit. So I would call her in Campeche from Vancouver, and we both would be yelling on the phone so that we could hear one another.

From 2000 to 2006, I visited with Mami every year, and sometimes we were fortunate to see each other even twice a year. In spite of our continued contact and the difficulty of trying to maintain closeness through phone calls, Mami always treated that goodbye at the airport as if it were the last one.

In the spring of 2007, Casa Lau was sold. Although the business had closed down in late 1989, it was only around 2003 that Mami discussed with Papito the idea of selling the actual building. During the following couple of years, word spread out in Tapachula that Casa Lau was on the selling block. Many people who knew Teti or of him, and what Casa Lau meant showed interest, but no solid offers came through. I myself toyed with the idea of buying it numerous times. However in the end, I chose to preserve Casa Lau's "foreverness" in my heart and in my mind, and to substitute the fragility of its physical structure with my own inspired memories and untouchable thoughts.

On a strange Monday in February 2007 during a business trip to Mexico, I received the dreaded yet unexpected phone call that Mami had died. She had almost made it to her ninetieth birthday, which would have been in May according to our western calendar and for which I had already planned a visit and purchased my plane ticket. What followed after that painful call has come back to me as something surreal, as one nightmare that I cannot seem to shake off easily: the long night I spent by myself at the hotel crying, the urgency to get to Campeche, the apprehension that came when I first caught a glimpse of Mami's casket, the feeling of regret for not forcing her to move to Vancouver so we could have spent more time together, the tears that would not stop running down my cheeks, the inability to convince my mind to stop the pain I felt in my heart, and the realization that this was indeed the last time I was seeing Mami.

But then I try to focus on the wife she was to Teti, on the mother she was to Papito and all her other children, and on the grandmother she was to me, my sisters, and cousins. And

I try to focus as well on all the important and difficult roles she played and was forced to play throughout her life as a woman and as a human being. For I think that to immortalize somebody is to remember the good.

I will never forget two incidents during my first visit with my husband to see Mami in Campeche. As usual, she never accepted the fact that for our holidays we so wished to see and spend time with her. Instead, she wanted my husband and me to enjoy our vacation by visiting as many tourist sites as possible. She hated sightseeing or going anywhere for that matter, but rode along everywhere knowing that we would not do anything without her. Also, she came to the conclusion that if she tagged along, it would maximize our brief time together. Thus, we drove everywhere together to make things more comfortable for everyone.

To make Mami's descent from Tía Lupe's van easier and softer, I would hold Mami's arm for support and my husband Pälle would place a cushion on the floor of the van. With a huge smile, she would land her bum on the cushion since her legs were terribly weak. Then, Pälle and I would hold one of her arms and pull her out of the car in unison. Every time we did this, she would burst out into contagious non-stop laughter, making us all laugh as well.

Three days later driving to Ciudad del Carmen, we stopped at a McDonald's for a soft ice cream cone because of the intense heat. Mami said to me she never ate ice cream because she never got *antojo* (craving for it). This time, I convinced her to try one. Then as we were leaving, Pälle asked Mami and me to sit on a bench. Quickly, my husband snapped a picture of a hysterically laughing Mami and a silly me sitting on the lap of a plastic statute of Ronald McDonald.

On both occasions as I was holding her arm to help her walk, Mami said to me that she had never laughed as much as she had with us. She said that, in fact, she rarely laughed at all then. With a calm expression she added, "Ah-Mey, I know now what it is to laugh out loud from the gut and to feel the elation of being happy. It is strange that I have gotten to experience total happiness in such a late period of my life. But I am lucky to have experienced it at all."

I am left thinking about the simplicity of her words in the midst of a complex but extraordinary life.

Mami and I in Ciudad del Carmen, Campeche (2002).

ABOUT THE AUTHOR

Born and raised in a small town in Mexico by Chinese parents and grandparents and working in the family grocery store surrounded by Cantonese and Spanish, I never considered life unusual. However, the more I observe and listen, read and travel, and meet people, the more I realize that my upbringing was not so ordinary. I am fascinated by the lenses through which we view the world, and the patterns and images that influence how we think about it and what it should look like. Isn't it odd and interesting at the same time to meet someone who looks Asian and speaks Spanish?

I currently live in Vancouver, British Columbia, and work at the University of British Columbia. *Mami: My Grandmother's Journey* is my first foray into the world of writing and publishing.